James Earley and Robert McArdle have written a book on the administrator's role that reads like an encyclopedia but exudes warmth and passion on almost every page. This impressive book brings the reader inside the important and mercurial world of special education, presenting a wealth of critical information while simultaneously speaking to the reader with unabashed candor and humility. It should be mandatory reading for all new administrators of special education.

—Charles Appelstein, MSW
Author, *No Such Thing as a Bad Kid: Understanding and Responding to Kids With Emotional and Behavioral Challenges Using a Positive, Strength-Based Approach*

This book is a professional gem. Grounded in integrity and keeping students at the forefront of their work, James Earley and Robert McArdle have created a practical guide on how to approach and manage the all-encompassing role of administrator of special education. Starting with a refresher on special education law and moving into a myriad of topics that fall under the responsibility of director, this resource is invaluable to all those working in the field of special education.

—Tamara (Tammy) Barrera, MEd
Assistant Director of Student Services

What a benefit to the larger community of special education administrators that, through this book, they can now access the collective knowledge and experience that James Earley and Robert McArdle have in the field. The role of the administrator of special education can be a lonely one and singular in its nature—the knowledge and skills required to do this job well are not often shared by anyone else in the district (not principals, nor curriculum directors, nor many superintendents). This book offers insight into all the role entails and how to lead the work.

—Alison Elmer, MEd
Special Education Director

It does not take long for the reader to realize that these seasoned special educators have the knowledge, skills, experience, and dispositions to provide a treasure trove of useful information for the novice or veteran whether they are a general education teacher, special education teacher, principal, superintendent, or special education administrator. James Earley and Robert McArdle leave no stone unturned and thoroughly address such topics as programs and services, discipline, budget development, professional development, supervision, and evaluation. This book is one you will want to keep close at hand.

—Stephen Gould, EdD
Program Director and Teacher at Lesley University,
Former Principal, and Former Assistant Superintendent

The special education administrator position is the most difficult job in public education. Challenges abound—conflicts with parents, teachers, and other administrators; changes to department of education regulations and guidance; litigation looming behind every decision—and perhaps the biggest, ever-present challenge is to balance advocacy for students with disabilities and the fiduciary responsibility to the school district. But help is on the way. Based on their extensive experience as special education directors, James Earley and Robert McArdle offer guidance in how to navigate the passage between the Scylla and Charybdis of conflicting demands, including tips and strategies for dealing with both the long-term and day-to-day challenges for special education directors. I highly recommend their book as a text in higher education courses, as an item in the library of special education organizations, and, most important, as a resource by the desk of every special education administrator.

—Edward McCaul, EdD
Keene State College, Former Special Education Administrator,
Former Executive Director of a Special Education Collaborative,
and Former Executive Director of Massachusetts
Administrators for Special Education

This succinct guidebook distills many years of practical experience and provides the reader with concrete guidance on the various aspects of the role of an administrator of special education; the authors not only address the anticipated issues associated with the position, but also weave in helpful advice on other potentially overlooked yet essential skills and actions necessary to be a successful administrator in public education. James Earley and Robert McArdle have provided an excellent resource that will help administrators of special education in confidently navigating the myriad issues to be addressed in that role.

—Thomas Nuttall, Esq.
Law Firm of Nuttall, MacAvoy, and Joyce PC

While the administering of special education can be a daunting task, authors James Earley and Robert McArdle, with their experience and expansive knowledge in special education administration, offer recommendations on how to work proactively with school administrators, special education and general education teachers, related services staff, parents, advocates, and other stakeholders. They share strategies that result in services that are responsive to student needs and the ever-present decision on placement in the educational setting in which the students can make effective educational progress. I enthusiastically recommend this book for school administrators, principals, and directors of special education schools, and as a text for undergraduate and graduate students in special education courses.

—Don Ricciato, PhD
Boston College, Lynch School of Education
and Human Development, Retired Director of the
Campus School at Boston College

There are no better administrators of special education than James Earley and Robert McArdle, and now, drawing on their decades of experience in special education leadership, they have created a thorough and practical guide that provides a wealth of information, useful advice, and, most important, ways to assess difficult situations and arrive at reasonable and equitable solutions. The book is a master class in identifying core issues and applying useful approaches to think about and solve many seemingly intractable problems. It is a book that is long overdue in the field and one that will have significant impact.

—Joel Ristuccia, MEd, CGS, MBA
Psychologist, School-Based Consultant, Coauthor,
Helping Traumatized Children Learn

This effort of our professional experiences is dedicated to our wives, Marlene and Maureen, for their support, encouragement, and ongoing willingness to listen to our conversations of stresses, successes, doubts, accomplishments, and desires for positive outcomes for school-age children with special needs.

A Practical Approach to Special Education Administration

Creating Positive Outcomes for Students With Different Abilities

James B. Earley
Robert J. McArdle

Foreword by Gerald Mazor

FOR INFORMATION:

Corwin
A SAGE Company
2455 Teller Road
Thousand Oaks, California 91320
(800) 233-9936
www.corwin.com

SAGE Publications Ltd.
1 Oliver's Yard
55 City Road
London EC1Y 1SP
United Kingdom

SAGE Publications India Pvt. Ltd.
B 1/I 1 Mohan Cooperative Industrial Area
Mathura Road, New Delhi 110 044
India

SAGE Publications Asia-Pacific Pte. Ltd.
18 Cross Street #10-10/11/12
China Square Central
Singapore 048423

President: Mike Soules
Vice President and Editorial Director:
  Monica Eckman
Publisher: Jessica Allan
Content Development Editor:
  Mia Rodriguez
Editorial Assistant: Natalie Delpino
Production Editor: Melanie Birdsall
Copy Editor: Melinda Masson
Typesetter: Exeter Premedia Services
Proofreader: Dennis Webb
Cover Designer: Candice Harman
Marketing Manager: Olivia Bartlett

Printed in Canada

ISBN 978-1-0718-7706-7

This book is printed on acid-free paper.

MIX
Paper from
responsible sources
FSC® C103567

22 23 24 25 26 10 9 8 7 6 5 4 3 2 1

Contents

Foreword

The special education administrator is one of the most challenging and visible positions in public education. In the mid-1970s, I completed my dissertation about this vital role, and I have watched it grow in importance and in influence ever since. I have seen it change and get more complicated over almost five decades.

James Earley, Robert McArdle, and I began our special education careers prior to the enactment of both the federal and state (Massachusetts) special education statutes in the early 1970s. The federal law (IDEA, formerly PL 94-142) was modeled after the Massachusetts statute. Throughout the past 50 years, special education has seen major modifications and refinements—due to court cases, landmark decisions, parental knowledge, research, amendments to existing legislation, medical breakthroughs, and educational trends—and the special education administrator has had to keep up with them all.

Jim and Bob have participated in and lived through these changes, and they bring to the table a combined century of experience. Since their retirement from public education more than 75 public school districts, educational collaboratives, and private schools for students with special needs have hired them to conduct special education program and district evaluations. In this capacity, they have interviewed, observed, or mentored administrators at every level—special education directors, out-of-district coordinators, building principals, superintendents, parents, teachers, ancillary service providers, and school committee members—and visited programs in public schools, educational collaboratives, and private schools.

A Practical Approach to Special Education Administration walks readers through the history of special education. The authors cover legal and regulatory issues, the importance of due process, and Section 504. They discuss helpful strategies for working not only with building and central office administrators but also parents, advocates, and teaching and ancillary staff. With a focus on program, budget, and professional development, they highlight techniques they have used with difficult cases, and what has worked for them.

It is fair to say that Jim and Bob have seen it all.

Whether you are new to special education administration or have many years of experience, reading this book will only make you better.

—Gerald Mazor, PhD

Retired Executive Director of the Concord Area Special Education (CASE) Collaborative, Concord, Massachusetts; and Former Interim Executive of the Lexington, Arlington, Burlington, Bedford, and Belmont (LABBB) Collaborative and LABBB Collaborative Consultant, Burlington, Massachusetts

Preface

As two veteran administrators of special education (ASEs) with 100+ years of professional experience in public, private, and nonprofit settings, we thought sharing our experience and experiences in a practical way would benefit current ASEs and those aspiring to the position. Although the position of ASE has seen some changes over the past 47 years, the primary role has not changed. Throughout our writing, we will take a practical approach to address some of the changes and their impacts. Over years of professional conversations supporting each other and our colleagues in various roles, we developed a strong sense that many ASEs were not fully prepared for the roles and expectations of the position. We felt that, even though over the years higher education had developed ASE training programs, the result was many sitting administrators lacking the complete preparedness and understanding required for the position, whose comprehensiveness and complexities can be and are at times overwhelming. Navigating the federal law and aspects of your state law, if you have one that differs from the federal law, can be challenging, to state the obvious. For example, Massachusetts services students through their 22nd birthday while the federal law—the Individuals With Disabilities Education Act (IDEA)—only services students through their 21st birthday. Other aspects of your state law, such as timeline compliance, may differ from the federal law, and you will need to know which standard your district is expected to meet. This book endeavors to equip those wanting to take on the challenge of becoming an ASE with a useful and practical guide to providing for the needs of students with disabilities.

As newly hired ASEs—we recognize the many different titles for this position, but for the purposes of this book, we will use administrator of special education (ASE)—we were given the privilege of overseeing programming and services for students in our school districts with special needs. With a great deal still to learn, we understood that many professionals within our district knew a whole lot more than we did about our responsibilities. We were also fortunate to learn from some of the pioneers at the state and local level, and like sponges we picked up every bit of advice, no matter how insignificant, to bring back to our districts.

So, we set out to meet every department member by visiting every school in the district and spending time in each classroom and specialist environment. We quickly learned that when we entered a school building, we came as outsiders, and that each school had its own culture, some more favorable to servicing students with special needs than others. We also realized that, to achieve success, we needed to prove ourselves to the staff and to the building administrator(s). Because building principals each led their school in a unique way, we needed to establish an individual relationship with each one, so we made sure, at every school, to stop first at the principal's office. In some schools, we found the principal in their office every time, and in other schools, we found the principal only after walking all around the school.

When one school had to close for several weeks due to mold, the fifth-grade students were placed at a middle school that happened to have one of those principals who never stayed in the office—to find this principal, you needed to traverse the school. One day, while walking down the corridor past the displaced class of fifth graders, the principal stopped to converse with the students, calling each by their name. When the class moved on, he was asked how he could possibly know all their names when they had only attended the school for a few weeks, and he responded, simply, "That's my job!" We came to understand that building principals, too, had a difficult job, and our job was not only to educate them on the new requirements of the laws but also to reveal ourselves as partners in the education of all students.

Some building administrators responded very positively while others did not. Convincing them to embrace our efforts and goals often proved difficult. So, after thinking a great deal about how to gain the staff's trust, we developed some not-so-earth-shattering routines.

Visibility

First, we cultivated *visibility*—not an easy task given the 24 schools in our respective districts serviced roughly 13,000 students, with 2,100 receiving special education services through an individualized education plan (IEP). In our first year, and throughout our tenure in various districts, we each read and signed every IEP, whether initial, annual review, or reevaluation, to see the writing style. If either of us had a question, we went to the school to discuss it with the liaison or team chairperson, and we made it a practice to visit with each special education staff member and building principal. These classroom visits also provided us a reminder of why we do this work: the students. Visiting their classrooms allowed us to meet the students and see their hard work as well as their teachers'. Without making time for these walk-throughs, you can very easily forget that each IEP you review or sign represents one student!

(As a point of observation, we realize that not all school districts are the same size, and you may not be able to connect with all your staff and building principals on a one-to-one and/or scheduled basis. We acknowledge that the size of the district will determine your ability to accomplish this direct contact. In larger districts with an organizational structure that includes middle managers for your department, you are responsible for delegating and establishing the visibility of these middle-level managers, assistant ASEs, program supervisors, and so on. In larger districts, delegation becomes an added skill that requires constant attention to ensure that the individuals charged with managerial responsibilities are fulfilling them as outlined in their job description.)

Listening

We also worked extremely hard to assure staff that we listened to their needs and wants. If we could not address them immediately, we made it a strict practice to tell the staff that we were not sure or did not know; however, we always got back to them within a day or two. So, we were becoming "visible," we were listening, and we were responding. If a staff member brought a sensitive issue to our attention, we took responsibility to address their concern without compromising them. This meant developing a strategy to achieve what we needed before presenting it to their school leader(s). We always felt that sharing our "strategy" with the building principal in a positive way would produce a positive outcome. In our separate roles, we attempted this throughout our careers as we also knew that if we did not "strategize" properly, then the special education students and staff could potentially take the brunt of our error.

Respect

Staff, district administrators, parents, and community leaders will observe you and scrutinize your approach. When we began in the position many years ago, two of our bosses shared with us their divergent advice on how to treat our staff and others. One advised us to respect everyone and treat your staff as professionals until they show you otherwise. The other advised us not to treat anyone with respect until they show you that they have earned it. Obviously, we are not aware of your leadership style or your approach to your staff and others. We can only tell you that we chose to treat everyone as a professional as we believed they had earned it through their training, experience, and dedication to the profession. We refrained from having anyone earn our respect. On some occasions, however, as we were advised, we did take responsibility to address someone whose actions were less than professional.

Responding

Years ago, a colleague advised us to wait 24 hours before reacting to a significant matter. We always attempted to follow that advice and give ourselves a day before addressing the individual or the correspondence. Though challenging, this step was critical for us to learn and practice throughout our careers. Especially for those "difficult conversations," we needed to bring our message forward as proactively as possible. Our approach? To look forward and refrain from looking back and asking the "why" questions. The best and simplest advice we can offer is to always use the five Ps: Prior Preparation Prevents Poor Performance.

ALWAYS REMEMBER

- Prior
- Preparation
- Prevents
- Poor
- Performance

Allowing ourselves time and remembering to prepare inevitably made the conversation or correspondence more proactive and productive. Following this process will prevent having to retract or modify what you may have stated otherwise. As a leader, you must always exhibit positive leadership, especially in difficult conversations with your staff, other school or district-based personnel, administrators, or parents.

We also believed that responding to parents was significantly important. If a parent contacted us, we were sure to get back to them as soon as possible, and we shared that same message with our staff—do not wait to respond to parents. For us, delaying a response to a parent is the same as delaying a response to a staff member; it sends the message that you do not believe their inquiry is important. That's why, as new ASEs, we always responded in a timely manner to let parents know we were interested in their concerns.

To this day, we are amazed that some (obviously very few) special education leaders view their staff as the enemy. We could never quite understand that. We always felt the staff were, in a way, our voice to students and parents as well as to their general education colleagues. We met with staff at least monthly as a group, and if we got a call from a staff member or a principal, in our respective district, we made sure to visit their building that day or the following morning on the way into work. In our role as a staff resource, we wanted to ensure that all staff felt comfortable in their own roles and knew and fully understood the requirements and our expectations for their jobs. For many years, we shared with staff the Leadership Lessons From Geese (Appendix I) at the beginning of the school year and let them know that together, we could rely on and learn from each other, and at any given time any one of us could take the lead on an issue or a project. We wanted our staff to know as much as if not more than we did, and that we too expected to learn from them.

We quickly realized that we also needed to learn a great deal about our districts and the people therein. This included school committee representatives, central office staff, building principals, the government of the community, and all the various special education staff within the district.

For example, one of us got a lesson in community and local government at a meeting in the mayor's office. When the mayor indicated that he had $100,000 for additional technology equipment, he was thanked, but informed that those funds could be better allocated to other, more pressing areas. He went on with the meeting but asked that I stay afterward, and proceeded to inform me that when the mayor offers you $100,000 for technology, you say thank you and move on—just one of the many political lessons that we learned.

To give you another example, years later, in the process of hiring a teaching assistant for a class, the final candidate was brought in front of the school committee for confirmation. One member began to react to the appointment of this individual, talking about nepotism, which surprised everyone, since the presence of such an issue was not previously indicated or disclosed, until the committee member revealed the individual's relation to one of the assistant superintendents. At that moment, we had an unpopular political decision to make. The committee was informed that this individual's relationship to the administrator was not previously disclosed, and that while our practice was to hire the best person for every position, we never asked about their relatives during interviews. When the committee confirmed the appointment with one vote opposed, it was obvious that "politically" a member of the committee was alienated. The process, however, reaffirmed the belief in hiring the individual who would best benefit the service to students within the district.

Like it or not, politics plays a role, and part of your job is to keep that in perspective. You work after all with the children of your community, and the funds to service these students come for the most part from local tax dollars, so you can expect to become immersed in politics at various times. As indicated, hold true to your beliefs, and if compromise is required on your part, ensure that your students and staff continue to receive what they require.

We have known a number of Superintendents that have said that the job of the Administrator of Special Education is the most difficult job in the school district. We tend to agree and when we have asked these Superintendents why, they explain that the job requires an aspect of every administrative job in the district budget, human resources, curriculum, assessment, transportation, interactions with staff, parents, students, all administrators, human service agencies, the department of education, legal (attorneys, advocates and hearing officers), school committee, and town/city leaders.

We learned early on that our biggest ally was allowing ourselves to *listen*. Most often staff and administrators had their own concerns, and note-taking allowed us to synthesize information so that when we did speak we were well informed. People need to be heard, and neither talking over them nor pushing our own agenda would give either of us the opportunity to listen. Keep in mind that listening requires comprehension and retention of the material presented while hearing merely implies that sounds have been received. It does not indicate comprehension or retention. One of us kept a saying on our desk—"I can explain it to you, but I can't understand it for you"—as a constant reminder that not everyone was going to fully understand our intentions and expectations. We would also remind ourselves that, according to research, people need to hear or do something 25 to 30 times before it becomes routine. Some will comply with your expectations right away, and others may need you to repeat them many times before they can internalize what you expect. Have you ever moved something, say from one drawer to another, only to repeatedly look for it in the old drawer before making a habit of finding it in the new drawer? When you change their expectations, staff, too, will keep going back to the old drawer! For some of the more important aspects of developing good listening skills, refer to Appendix II.

About the Authors

James B. Earley, EdD, is an independent special education consultant, contracted for the LABBB Collaborative, the SEEM Collaborative, the Northshore Education Consortium, and Seaside Educational Consultants. He has 52 years of public education experience as a teacher, teaching assistant principal, and Massachusetts Department of Education supervisor and acting regional special education director; nearly 30 years as administrator of special education and interim superintendent of schools for the Watertown Public Schools; and 12 years as managing director of Walker Partnerships prior to assuming his current consulting activities. Dr. Earley has been a senior lecturer at Lesley University and Wheelock College, an adjunct professor at the University of Massachusetts Boston, and a student teacher supervisor for Salem State University. Dr. Earley has consulted for numerous educational organizations, has participated in a variety of special education task forces and committees, and was a member of the Executive Board of the Massachusetts Administrators for Special Education for 24 years. He has conducted over 125 independent program reviews and evaluations for public schools, private special education schools, and charter schools. He has conducted numerous professional development trainings for school districts within Massachusetts and several other states. He has been recognized for his contributions to the field of special education and received several awards, culminating with being named the 2003 Outstanding Administrator of Special Education by the Council of Administrators of Special Education. He received his bachelor's in education and his master's in education, social rehabilitation administration, from Northeastern University in Boston; his Certificate of Advanced Graduate Study (CAGS) in organizational and administrative theory at Boston University; and his doctorate in education, with an emphasis on educational leadership, from the University of Massachusetts Amherst.

 **Robert J. McArdle, MEd,** is an independent special education consultant with over 47 years in public education as a mediator and educational specialist for the Office of Elementary and Secondary Education, administrator of special education for Woburn Public Schools, pupil personnel administrator for the Greater Lawrence Technical School and Stoneham Public Schools, executive director of the Greater Lawrence Educational Collaborative and the Gifford School, and Northeast associate manager of Walker Partnerships. Mr. McArdle has been a visiting faculty member at Salem State University, Fitchburg State University, the University of Massachusetts Boston, and Endicott College. He has served in several interim positions and has mentored both public and private school administrators. Mr. McArdle has conducted over 70 public school special education program evaluations and has served on numerous advisory boards, task forces, and special committees. He has presented at numerous conferences and conducted professional training sessions for school personnel for over 40 years. Mr. McArdle has served in several executive board positions, including president of the Massachusetts Administrators for Special Education. He is also a past recipient of the Massachusetts Special Education Administrator of the Year Award.

Practice is the best of all instructors.
—Diogenes Laërtius (c. 200 CE)

Introduction

When we started writing back in February 2020, little did we know what situation we would be in today—stay-at-home orders, millions out of work, schools closed, and teachers providing virtual learning. As educational leaders go about training, setting new policies, and assisting their staff, we are reminded of a 1989 presentation by Joel Barker: "When a paradigm shifts," he indicates, "everyone goes back to zero."

It brings us back to 1974 and the implementation of Massachusetts Chapter 766. Everyone was working to understand the regulatory requirements, establish programs, determine appropriate assessment tools, learn how to conduct team meetings, develop budgets for unanticipated expenditures, and on and on. And there we were in 2020, in an almost identical situation—educational leaders attempting to determine requirements, establish service options and opportunities, decide on appropriate assessment, run virtual team meetings, and on and on. Once again, how do we educate individuals with disabilities and ensure that they receive a free appropriate education . . . *virtually*? The new laws in Massachusetts and at the federal level introduced an array of requirements that clearly marked a paradigm shift in services for students with special needs in public schools. Everyone—teachers, students, parents, administrators, and school committees—had to start at zero understanding of how to go about decision making and providing services to identified students. The same can be said for education in the COVID-19 era: Both general and special educators started at zero understanding of how to provide virtual as well as safe in-person instruction.

Using an example of an environment that we are completely familiar with, the school year in 1974 Massachusetts opened unlike any before as the new law, Chapter 766, would be implemented in all school districts across the Commonwealth. Many school leaders, parents, advocates, and special interested community members questioned how school districts would go about meeting the demands of the new law. Few had any idea how the law would play out as the years progressed. The law, initially titled the Bartley-Daly Act after the two legislators that authored it, was intended to ensure that students with special needs, as they were referred to, received an education in the least restrictive environment. To address this, the regulations written to implement the law contained so-called program prototypes. Loosely based on Maslow's (1954) hierarchy of needs, the prototypes indicated the placement for students found eligible for special education. Maslow's hierarchy is a motivational theory in psychology comprising a five-tier model of human needs, often depicted as levels within a pyramid. From the bottom of the hierarchy upwards, the needs are physiological (food and clothing), safety (job security), love and belonging (friendship), esteem, and self-actualization. Needs lower down in the hierarchy must be satisfied before individuals can attend to needs higher up.

All prototypes began with 502 (the regulation section number of the law), with a 502.1 prototype being placement in regular education with monitoring by a special educator, and continued from there up to 502.11 as follows:

502.2 Placement in special education for up to 25% of the school day

502.3 Placement in special education from 25% to 60% of the school day

502.4 Placement in special education from 60% to 100% of the school day

502.4i Placement in a separate approved program, sometimes off site in a separate school building

502.5 Placement in an approved private day school

502.6 Placement in an approved private residential school

502.7 Placement in a home or hospital setting

502.8 Placement in a preschool program

502.10 Placement in an off-site alternative program

502.11 Placement for students 16 years an older, alternative program

The regulations covered "mainstreaming," the amount of time a student spent in the regular education classroom. The law initially intended to allow students with significant disabilities to participate in the regular education environment to the maximum extent possible. The regulations, when drafted and implemented, were quite extensive (207 pages) and included various timelines for school districts to meet as well as the formal process to be utilized in determining a student's eligibility.

The new law in Massachusetts, enacted one year before the federal law serving children with disabilities—PL 94-142 (1975), now the Individuals With Disabilities Education Act (IDEA)—was signed into law, meant that regular education teachers would play a significant role in servicing the needs of eligible students. Many felt they lacked the training to accomplish this and that the special educators, who at the time required certification in both regular and special education, needed to take on the bulk of the responsibility for their students. Hindsight being what it is, we now see that pulling eligible students from their regular classroom may not have been the most prudent way to proceed. In fact, with the inclusion movement of today, many consider such pulling out as segregating. Nonetheless, school districts found themselves in the position of developing new programs to meet the needs of students deemed eligible based on standardized assessments and the determination of the evaluation team.

All these new requirements needed overseeing, and many administrators of special education (ASEs) came from the ranks of school psychologists, guidance personnel, special education teachers, special education program supervisors, speech and language pathologists, and even elementary principals with some background in special education.

No programs were available at the time of implementation of the law and regulations, whose idea of specifically training an ASE candidate to do the job was "figure it out as you go." While today some colleges and universities offer educational leadership programs with a focus on special education, in the early years strong collaboration developed in our state, and collaboratives brought together ASEs from different local school districts into a special education network on a regular basis to provide programs and services for low-incident students. We always viewed collaborative programs as an extension of the public schools working to mirror our district's curriculum and the state curriculum frameworks for the population of students receiving services. The state's department of education also held monthly meetings to assist ASEs, executive directors of special education collaboratives, and executive directors of private special needs schools in understanding the new landscape. All of this was beneficial for understanding the new law, regulations, and policies that flowed from the regulations; however, it did not lend itself to implementing the law or the regulations in local school districts or individual schools.

We are sure that, once in the position, you'll understand the extent of your responsibility to every parent, teacher, administrator, paraprofessional, secretary, and public official in your city or town. Everything that goes wrong may ultimately get blamed on your department, such as budget overruns, high-stakes and standardized test standings (within the district and at each building), and even staffing levels. So how do you succeed in this position? Each day as we went off to work, we felt like we were juggling 100 balls in the air, and we also knew that as we attempted to keep them all suspended, we would get 500 questions from parents, staff, and administration. We considered it a good day if we answered 50% of the questions correctly and still had most of the balls in the air. No two days were ever the same, and it always felt like we needed more hours to get the job done. When the day appears to pace at breakneck speed, however, it is important to allow yourself to reflect on any difficult decisions you're required to make.

As indicated, a former colleague stands out for reminding us to "sleep on it"—that is, for any significant matter involving personnel, an individual school, a parent, or an administrator, such as letters, emails, texts, or negative information brought to our attention by word of mouth, we would take a full 24 hours, holding back no matter how great a need to respond immediately, to prepare our response and think through potential ramifications and unintended consequences—an approach that not only gave us time to process our response, but also allowed us to gauge the urgency to respond. Is a matter really so urgent as to require immediate response, or is it important enough for you to double-check all the facts before responding to ensure you accurately address the issue?

Today, this appears to be even more important given cell phones, email, and text. Everyone wants an immediate response, so before you send that email or respond to that text, allow yourself the time to consider the most productive way to respond. Just as important, remind yourself that "there is no such thing as an educational emergency." If a student climbs a tree and refuses to come down or runs from the classroom and school, it might be an emergency; however, at that moment, it does not have much to do with education. Bottom line? Educational matters can wait until tomorrow. We heard many times over the years from new ASEs how everyone expects you to be available. As indicated, you have taken on a position that makes you responsible for all aspects of special education within your district and to the many constituents with a vested interest. It is not uncommon for several individuals to expect that you will be available to hear their thoughts and concerns. Your challenge is to prioritize the requests by importance and to always respond by indicating when you can speak or meet with the individual who raised the issue. As part of this challenge, you need to be aware of how people might receive your response. If they interpret your message as putting them off or not taking them seriously, you may be causing something small to become something big. Once again, you must fall back on the five *P*s and work to ensure that your message is received in a positive and proactive manner.

We gained valuable insight from staff, parents, principals, custodians, paraprofessionals, and colleagues from other districts in the same position. However, we must admit that some of our best advice came from our secretaries—the people who interacted with everyone both inside and outside the school district. In conversations with our secretaries, the individuals mentioned would often share a great deal that they never shared with us, and we learned that before putting anything out to staff or parents, we needed to check in with our secretaries to assess their reaction to the content. We encouraged their feedback, and often they shared insight into how staff might receive the information or how parents might interpret the message.

If you have mentors or coaches, and we hope that you do, listen to them, whoever they may be. When we began in the position, coaching and mentoring were not viewed as a necessity as they are today. We did, however, have individuals who provided us guidance, and as we look back, we recognize them as our mentors and coaches. Simply stated, a coach tries to direct a person to some end result, and a mentor serves as a sounding board for the individual. You need to identify where in the job performance you may need assistance and seek it out, whether from a colleague in the district, a counterpart in another district, or a consultant contracted solely to mentor or coach you.

One of us had a mentor years ago who happened to be a previous boss. He sent me to a training on mental health, and when I returned, I made an appointment to see him and share what I had learned—only to be informed that he would wait to hear me share it at the next staff meeting. When I responded, "*What?* I can't do that," he said, "Sure you can! After all, you are the duty expert; you were there, and they were not." To this I responded, "What if they ask me something I cannot answer?" and he said, "Tell them you will check into that and get back to them." So, from that point on, we envisioned ourselves as duty experts, and we knew that if someone asked us a question, we would simply let them know that we'd consider it and circle back with an answer. As the special education "duty expert" in your district, you, too, must be sure to provide an answer to those questions.

Another time we reached out to a mentor, he said, "Oh, I am so glad you called! All these staff members keep coming to my door, every one of them with an 'albatross on their back'"—an idiom that refers to a heavy burden someone carries—"and you know what they want me to do? They want me to feed the albatross. They don't know that it is my job to *teach* them how to feed the albatross." This may be a crude way of looking at it, but all too often when people come to our doors with a problem, we make it our job to take it on rather than teaching them how to address it. Student, parent, communication, or building issues—we need to assist the individuals who raise them while resisting the temptation to solve their problems for them, which often would prove so much easier.

A final point shared by one of our mentors: One day, he was told that the list of to-dos up on the office wall seemed like a million things, all equally doable and important and certainly overwhelming. The ASE's job, he advised, was to prioritize *the one, most important thing* and do that, then prioritize the next thing, and so on. You can only do one thing at a time, so select the most important priority, finish it, then move to the next, and before you know it not only will very few things remain on that wall, but your sense of overwhelming will certainly lessen.

So, if you want to become an ASE, let us share some of what we learned throughout our careers. As you proceed through these chapters, we believe that the information they contain will provide a sound and practical foundation for aspiring and current ASEs alike. We hope that much of what we learned, and a few mistakes we made, will assist ASEs at every level to move forward in the many demanding areas of their position, allowing them to be effective as both administrators and educational leaders.

PART I

Foundational Elements

1

Legal Foundation for Providing a Free and Appropriate Education to Students With Disabilities

The purpose of this chapter is to provide a greater awareness and understanding of why we do what must be done in special education. Court decisions have established the legal framework for how to provide for students with disabilities and other special needs. According to Burrello and Sage (1979), "As part of the social climate of the times, and as a reflection of adversarial relations, the increasing intervention of the courts into determination of specifics of social change constitutes a force of such significance as to warrant consideration in its own right" (p. 36).

The continually debated issue is whether current special education legislation at the state and federal level counts as civil rights legislation or education reform legislation. In the opinion of many practitioners, it is both, with the emphasis on civil rights based on numerous court decisions beginning with *Plessy v. Ferguson* in 1896. This U.S.

Supreme Court decision advanced the controversial "separate but equal" doctrine of racial segregation. Although the majority opinion did not contain the phrase, it gave constitutional sanction to laws designed to achieve racial segregation and served as a controlling judicial precedent until 1954.

That's the year the Supreme Court decided *Brown v. Board of Education of Topeka*, a landmark case in which the justices ruled unanimously that racial segregation in public schools was unconstitutional. *Brown* was one of the cornerstones of the civil rights movement and helped establish the precedent that "separate but equal" education and other services are not, in fact, equal at all.

In this case, which would become famous, Oliver Brown filed a class-action suit against the Board of Education of Topeka, Kansas, in 1951, after his daughter, Linda Brown, was denied entrance to Topeka's all-white elementary schools. The court stated, "In these days, it is doubtful that any child may reasonably be expected to succeed in life if he is denied the opportunity of an education. Such an opportunity, where the state has undertaken to provide it, is a right which must be made available to all on an equal term."

This decision employed the concept of equal rights as derived from the Fourteenth Amendment, which prohibits discrimination against a class of persons for an arbitrary or unjustified reason—"No State shall make or enforce any law which shall abridge the privileges or immunities of citizens of the United States; nor shall any State deny any person of life, liberty, or property, without due process of law; nor deny to any person within its jurisdiction the equal protection of the laws"—and applied it to a particular minority group. What is significant with regard to the Fourteenth Amendment is its focus on ensuring civil rights and services to a group or class of individuals. Although the case had nothing to do with special education, it did set the precedent that separate is *not* equal, and many future courts would use *Brown* as the foundation for their decisions.

Inarguably, special education legislation is about equal access and due process for students with disabilities. Prior to 1940, public school districts across the United States provided little if any special education services. Some states provided institutional programs for certain disability categories but little in the way of comprehensive programming, especially at the local level. Through the 1940s and 1950s, while incremental steps were occurring at the state and local level, no requirements for special education services were yet in place. Gradually, through the 1960s, states and local school districts began to respond to social pressure as an outgrowth of the civil rights movement, equal opportunity concerns, and education for all as rendered through a sampling of the following court decisions.

1965—PL 89–10, the Elementary and Secondary Education Act (ESEA), provided a comprehensive plan for readdressing the inequality of educational opportunity for economically underprivileged children and became the statutory basis upon which early special education legislation was drafted. ESEA also provided federal funding to improve the education of certain categories of children, including children with disabilities.

1966—Title VI was added to ESEA, funding grants for children with disabilities.

1969—In *Wolf v. State Legislature of Utah*, the Utah Supreme Court ruled that children with intellectual disabilities had the right to attend public school. The court further ruled that admission to public school could not be denied to a student due to the student's intellectual disability. Echoing *Brown*, the court also affirmed that no "child may reasonably be expected to succeed in life if he is denied the opportunity of an education." The Utah court further ruled that "Segregation of the plaintiff children from public school system unusually interpreted as denoting their inferiority, unusualness, uselessness, and incompetency" and that "even though, perhaps well intention, under the apparent sanction of law and state authority has a tendency to retard the educational, emotional and mental development of the children." Interestingly, this particular court case is the basis for much of the research on inclusion that has occurred since the early 1970s.

1971—*Wyatt v. Stickney* saw the Alabama Supreme Court rule that students in state-operated and -funded institutions have a right to treatment, including habilitation, transportation, and education in the Least Restrictive Environment (LRE) with due regard for privacy and other basic attributes of human living. This ruling set detailed standards for treatment with an emphasis on LRE.

1972—In *Mills v. Board of Education of District of Columbia*, the court ruled that the school system "failed to provide a public education for all types of handicapped, disturbed and retarded children," which led to the following orders:

- Services for students identified as having special needs must be offered within 30 days.

- Hearing procedures must be established to guard against the indiscriminate suspension, exclusion, or placement of pupils in special education programs.

- Economic excuses for not implementing special education programs must not be used.

The ruling from the *Mills* case inspired the filing of litigation in a number of states dealing with related issues:

- Open access to education.

- No rejection regardless of a student's intellectual or physical condition.

- Use of a single test or assessment results (IQ) as the main criteria for placing a student in substantially separate classes.

- Entitling parents and children to be heard regarding the appropriateness of the education assignment.

1972—Following *Mills*, in *Pennsylvania Association of Retarded Citizens v. Commonwealth of Pennsylvania*, the Pennsylvania Supreme Court ruled on two significant issues:

- Every child with intellectual disabilities is capable of deriving benefits from an education.

- In addition to the equal protection concept, the Fourteenth Amendment includes the Due Process Clause, the primary guaranteed basis for the development of procedural rights for the parents of children with intellectual disabilities.

In sum, no child eligible for a publicly supported education could be denied such education without an equal alternative tailored to the child's needs, and the district's practice of excluding children with disabilities from education was deemed unlawful. The judge ordered the district to take the following actions:

- To provide accessible, free, and suitable education for all children of school age regardless of disability or impairment.

- To not suspend a child for more than two days without a hearing.

- To provide all parties in the suit with publicly supported educational programs tailored to their needs.

This trend eventually led to important federal policies such as the Education for All Handicapped Children Act of 1974, which finally made free public education a reality for many children who had previously been denied this right.

1972—Massachusetts passed the first special education law, the Bartley-Daly Act, in 1972. Implemented in 1974, the law became commonly known as Chapter 766, and it was the first to focus specifically on special education students in the United States. Chapter 766 was a noncategorical law, and it is interesting to note that it took 20 years from the *Brown* decision for a law to be written to protect the rights of students with disabilities, with a primary focus on their civil rights.

1974—The U.S. Supreme Court case of *Lau v. Nichols* saw the court rule that refusing to provide English learners with supplemental language courses violated the California Education Code and Section 601 of the Civil Rights Act of 1964. The unanimous decision pushed public schools to develop plans to increase the linguistic skills of students for whom English was a second language.

The same year brought PL 93-380, the Education Amendments of 1974, which established two laws:

- The Education of the Handicapped Act Amendments of 1974, the first mention of an appropriate education for all children with disabilities.
- The Family Educational Rights and Privacy Act (FERPA), giving parents (and students over the age of 18) the right to examine records in a student's personal file.

1975—The federal law PL 94-142, the Education for All Handicapped Children Act, was passed in 1975. This law mandated a free appropriate public education for all children with disabilities, including Individualized Education Plans (IEPs), LRE, and due process rights, and became the basis for federal funding of special education. The law was renamed the Individuals With Disabilities Education Act (IDEA) in 1990.

President Gerald Ford had many thoughts regarding the 1975 law; he viewed certain features of the law as objectionable and thought they should be changed. Some of his comments included the following:

- "Unfortunately, this bill promises more than the Federal Government can deliver, and its good intentions could be thwarted by the many unwise provisions it contains."

- "It contains a vast array of detailed, complex, and costly administrative requirements."

- "It establishes complex requirements under which tax dollars would be used to support administrative paperwork and not educational programs."

- "Unfortunately, these requirements will remain in effect even though the Congress appropriates far less than the amounts contemplated in [PL 94-142]."

- "Fortunately, since the provisions of this bill will not become fully effective until fiscal year 1978, there is time to revise the legislation and come up with a program that is effective and realistic."

Many of Ford's concerns continue to ring true today—in particular, costly administrative requirements, time-consuming administrative paperwork, lack of federal appropriation, and ultimately no changes prior to implementation. Paperwork and compliance concern all teachers and administrators, and yet the promise of the law reimbursing school districts 40% of all special education expenditures has never been met, instead varying between 15% and 18%.

1975—*Goss v. Lopez* was another case brought before the U.S. Supreme Court in 1975. In this case, nine students at two high schools and one junior high school in Columbus, Ohio, received 10-day suspensions from school. The school principals did not hold hearings for the affected students before ordering the suspensions, and Ohio law did not require them to do so. The principals' actions were challenged nonetheless, and a federal court found that the students' rights had been violated. The case was then appealed to the Supreme Court. In terms of relevancy for school disciplinary hearings, did the imposition of the suspensions without preliminary hearings violate the students' due process rights as guaranteed by the Fourteenth Amendment? The court answered that, yes, it did.

In a 5-to-4 decision, the court held that because Ohio had chosen to extend the right to an education to its citizens, it could not withdraw that right "on grounds of misconduct absent fundamentally fair procedures to determine whether the misconduct ha[d] occurred." The court held that Ohio was constrained to recognize students' entitlement to education as property interests protected by the Due Process Clause that could not be taken away without minimum procedures required by the clause. In addition, the court found that students facing suspension should at a minimum be given notice and afforded some kind of hearing. *Goss* stands for the basic principle that a due process hearing is required for any student facing a long-term suspension (i.e., suspension of 10 days or more) or exclusion.

1982—The question of free and appropriate education was addressed in *Board of Education of the Hendrick Hudson Central School District v. Rowley*. The court clarified that the free and appropriate education must "permit the child educationally to benefit from the instruction" and must be reasonably calculated to allow the student to attain passing grades and annual promotion. In the decision, the court held that "free appropriate is the floor" when determining student progress.

1984—In *Stock v. Massachusetts Hospital School*, the court required the Massachusetts Department of Education to administer special education programs "to assure the maximum possible development of a child with special needs." This case moved Massachusetts to the standard of maximum rather than appropriate and was future elaborated upon a year later in the *David D.* case.

1985—*David D.* reiterated that "free and appropriate is the floor"; however, the court indicated that the federal law stated "the child's education will meet the standard of the state educational agency." The language in Massachusetts Chapter 766 was for a child to be educated to the "maximum feasible benefit."

1985—That same year, *Burlington School Committee v. Massachusetts Department of Education* saw the court reimburse parents for a unilateral placement. This case began at the Bureau of Special Education Appeals (BSEA) where the hearing officer found in favor of the parents. The Burlington Public Schools took the result to the U.S.

Court of Appeals for the First Circuit, which overturned the BSEA decision and ordered parents to reimburse the local education agency (LEA). The parents appealed the decision of the circuit court to the Supreme Court, which found in their favor and remanded the decision back to the circuit court for resolution. This decision had a significant impact on compliance and timelines as the court found the parents' "self-help" unilateral placement justified due to the district not meeting compliance requirements.

1988—*Honig v. Doe* is a U.S. Supreme Court decision that dealt with the issue of expelling a child with disabilities based on actions arising from the child's disability. The court ruled that a school district may not unilaterally exclude or expel a child with disabilities from the classroom for any dangerous or disruptive conduct resulting from the child's disabilities, and created what is now known as the "10-day rule," which allows a school to only suspend a child for up to 10 days without parental consent or court intervention. Finally, the court ruled that students could not be removed from school if the behavior they exhibited was a result of their disability.

1988—In the *Timothy W. v. Rochester, New Hampshire, School District* case, the U.S. District Court for New Hampshire ruled that even children with the most severe disabilities meet the statutory requirements for special education services. This ruling established the "zero reject" policy—that all children, regardless of the severity of their disability, are entitled to an education.

1990—PL 101-476, the Education of the Handicapped Act (another precursor to IDEA), added several new elements; among them, it expanded and reauthorized discretionary programs, mandated transition services, defined assistive technology devices and services, and added autism and traumatic brain injury to the list of disability categories.

1993—A West Virginia circuit court (Civil Action No. 92-C-92) heard the only case, *Doe v. Withers*, of a teacher being held personally responsible for violating the civil rights of a student with special needs. The facts of the case involve a student diagnosed with a learning disability whose IEP allowed for oral testing with a special education teacher in a resource room throughout middle school. When the student entered high school in September, the student's parents met with all teachers, and all but one agreed to the testing in the resource room. That teacher, Mr. Withers, administered nine tests without allowing the student to go to the resource room, and further belittled the student in class in front of other students. The parents then asked to meet with Mr. Withers again, but he refused, and the student, who failed the class, was not allowed to participate in extracurricular activities. At the midpoint of the school year, Mr. Withers left his position to become a state legislator, and when a substitute teacher replaced him, the student's grades improved dramatically with the opportunity for oral testing. The student's parents filed a civil rights violation requesting compensatory damages against Mr. Withers for $30,000, the principal for $10,000, the superintendent for $10,000, and the school board for $10,000.

The court granted relief to the principal, superintendent, and school board based on efforts made to assist Mr. Withers to comply with the student's IEP. The jury, however, ruled in favor of the student and parents, and ordered Mr. Withers to pay the following:

- $5,000 in compensatory damages.
- $10,000 in punitive damages.
- Interest back to the filing date of the action and all costs related to the action.

1994—In *Sacramento City Unified School District v. Rachel H.*, the district court found that defendant Rachel Holland received substantial benefits in regular education and that all her IEP goals could be implemented in a regular classroom with some modification to the curriculum and the assistance of a part-time aide. While the school district had consistently taken the view that a child with Rachel's IQ (41) had too severe of intellectual disabilities to benefit from full-time placement in a regular classroom, the Hollands maintained that Rachel learned both social and academic skills in a regular classroom and would not benefit from placement in special education. The school district appealed this determination to the district court.

Also in 1994, the Ninth Circuit Court of Appeals reiterated two earlier circuit court decisions by applying four factors to determine whether a placement meets the LRE requirements of IDEA:

- The student's educational benefit from full-time placement in a regular education classroom.
- The nonacademic benefits of a regular classroom placement.
- Effect of the child with a disability on the rest of the class.

- The cost of a regular education placement with proper supplemental aids and service.

Three other federal district courts have affirmed these standards, which apply to 18 states. This case has long been referenced as the precursor to full inclusion, although the court did not indicate how to define or interpret the four determining factors.

1999—The U.S. Supreme Court decision in *Cedar Rapids Community School District v. Garret F.* adopted the bright-line, physician/nonphysician approach to health services that school districts must provide intensive, one-on-one nursing services. The court held to *Tatro's* bright-line decision to determine if a service is medical or related. (*Irving Independent School District v. Tatro* is a 1984 case in which the court affirmed granting the parents of a child with disabilities the right to medical procedures as part of her IEP.)

2002—The Massachusetts legislature voted to adopt the federal standard of free and appropriate education. As noted earlier, the Massachusetts standard had been established in *David D.* as maximum feasible benefit. Massachusetts further required all teachers to be "highly qualified" and began utilizing the federal categories. The Massachusetts laws had been noncategorical since the implementation 18 years earlier of Chapter 766.

2004—PL 108-446, the Individuals With Disabilities Education Act of 2004 (IDEA), did all of the following:

- Attempted to align with No Child Left Behind (NCLB).
- Defined highly qualified special education teacher.
- Expanded dispute resolution options.
- Provided access to instructional materials.
- Allowed IDEA funds to be used for early intervening services to serve students not IDEA eligible.
- Ensured services for unhoused students and students attending private schools along with highly mobile students.

2017—In *Endrew F. v. Douglas County School District*, the U.S. Supreme Court's decision addressed the substantive standard for the central obligation under IDEA of a Free and Appropriate Public Education (FAPE).

The court had not revisited this issue for 35 years, having originally addressed it in the landmark IDEA case *Board of Education of Hendrick Hudson Central School District v. Rowley*, and issued its decision with a refinement of the *Rowley* standard. Starting with the *Rowley* language, the court added a more individualized predicate: "a school must offer an IEP reasonably calculated to enable a child to make progress appropriate in light of the child's circumstances."

CHAPTER SUMMARY

The cases described in this chapter have shaped the framework for special education across the United States. Among the numerous cases brought to clarify aspects of both state and federal laws, including Irving Independent School District v. Amber Tatro, 468 U.S. 883 (1984) (where the court affirmed granting the parents of a child with disabilities the right to medical procedures as part of her IEP), and *Cedar Rapids v. Garret F., 526 U.S. 66 (1999)* (where the court affirmed providing continuous one-on-one nursing services for the respondent student), these decisions established the guidance for individual state legislatures and eventually the federal legislature to put into law the right to a free and appropriate education in the LRE, which can be a regular education classroom if the student can receive a satisfactory education in that setting. When appropriate, education should be provided at the local level and must always be based on the learning needs of the individual student. These educational services must be provided within a reasonable time regardless of cost. The system developed for identifying students must not discriminate, and while a full range of programming must be available to provide the required services to the identified student, these services must be reviewed and reevaluated periodically, which requires parental permission and due process, through a third party.

After 58 years from *Plessy* to *Brown*, 18 years from *Brown* to the implementation of Chapter 766, and 2 years from Chapter 766 to PL 94-142, more court cases are likely to shape the future direction of the provision of services for students who require a special education. It is important to remember that we are still in the infancy stages of these laws, and, clearly, more changes in medical diagnoses, assessment protocols, educational initiatives, and evidenced-based practices are to come. We will also see more challenges to the law and various regulations that continue to shift how we currently view our role.

The administrator of special education is responsibile for presenting these facts, representing a course of action to ensure a free and appropriate education in the LRE for students identified with special needs within their school districts.

2 Defining Your Beliefs

When we entered the field of special education administration, we soon realized the need to identify, in our own terms, our beliefs regarding services for children between the ages of 3 and 21 or 22 with special needs. We needed to articulate to the school community, including administrators, school committees, the surrounding community, parents, and special education staff, what was driving our work, and we recognized that our personal values as individuals, educators, and administrators were the foundation of our beliefs. Let's say we wanted our mission statement to encompass all our previous life and professional experiences that had driven our practice, in our various positions, throughout our careers. It is so crucial, looking back, that we were able to articulate these beliefs; they kept us from compromising as we moved through our work, in the many positions we held over many years.

We can say that borrowing from other sources framed the language of our thoughts, beliefs, and actions. Beyond ensuring a Free and Appropriate Public Education (FAPE) in the Least Restrictive Environment (LRE) for all identified students, we developed additional beliefs:

- All children *can* learn.
- All children have the right to be treated as typical (the right to be regular).

- All children must have access to learning in the least restrictive setting.

- All children can and should be held to high standards and expectations.

- School-based staff and parents must be listened to and supported.

- Special education laws have allowed our society to think inclusively.

- All individuals have different needs and abilities, and all of us can embrace diversity.

- All school-age children deserve respect and attention to their needs, and adults must do what is best for these children and provide for their needs.

We must make a unified commitment to ensure through our authority as administrators of special education (ASEs) that a FAPE is provided in the LRE to all students determined to require special education services. As educators and administrators, we have made a concerted effort to develop programs and services that allow students with special needs to develop to their full potential. Our primary focus has always been the student; if we focused on what a student required, we believed, we would never go wrong. Taking actions and making decisions in the best interest of students based on evaluation data, plus evidence-based practice, is a formula for eventual student success.

Laurence M. Lieberman, in his 2001 article "The Death of Special Education," considered whether "disability equals failure" or "failure equals disability." We, too, grappled with this question throughout our careers; what if a student simply chooses to fail should we suspect a disability? Lieberman believed that when a student fails, the system fails, and further felt that focusing on the student was counterproductive to seeking student change while neglecting system change. He shared several other strong beliefs—for example, that general education teachers and principals had a responsibility to accommodate for all students, that a strong prereferral process and intervention activities should be required before considering a student for referral to special education, and that the law has "very little to do with either individuals or disabilities"; rather, Lieberman suggested, "it has become the At-Risk for Failure in the Regular Classroom Act."

At the secondary level we would, on occasion, have students who chose not to attend their special education services, and when this occurred, the staff sought to "write them out" of special education services. When we became aware of this, we informed staff that missing class did not make the student's disability go away. They first needed to contact the parents, and if that was not successful, they would need to reconvene the Team. In situations like this, it is important that you take a proactive lead; while staff may not be happy as it would be easier to discontinue the services, it is your responsibility to protect the district and the student's right to an education. If services were stopped, the parent or student could come back to the district in the future claiming that a FAPE was not provided. Rather than take that chance, we advised staff that if after the Team meeting the student still failed to attend, then the student's Individualized Education Plan (IEP) should be sent to the state as a rejection. By doing this, we acknowledged that the student continued to be eligible for and require services, and we would look toward due process to resolve the matter. As we went about our work, we would always think of the worst-case scenario: Were we putting ourselves in a position that we might not be able to defend? We were also known to say "document, document, document" as we always wanted to make sure we had the required information to back up any action we might take. With all the requirements of special education, be it paperwork, timelines, or other notifications, we knew that documenting that the requirement had been met would potentially elevate concerns in the future.

We will address professional development and your responsibility to provide current and up-to-date information to all your staff in Chapter 10. Meanwhile, some simple reminders can have a lasting impact on staff as well. Many of you may be familiar with the song, written and performed by the late Harry Chapin, "Flowers Are Red." We often shared it with staff and administrators as well as students we had the pleasure of teaching in our college courses as it sends a strong, emotional message about the impact of adults on the education of children. The song is about a little boy who goes to school seeing all the colors of the rainbow, and during art time, he draws flowers in a spectrum of colors. When the teacher asks him what he is doing, he tells her he's "painting flowers," but the teacher explains that flowers are red and leaves are green and that is how they have always been. Still, the little boy continues to paint flowers in all the colors of the rainbow, and soon the teacher has had enough and puts him in a corner, saying it is for his own good and he must not come out until he gets it right and responds as he should. Frightening stories do not take long to fill his head, and soon the boy approaches the teacher and agrees that "flowers are red and leaves are green." Time goes by as it always does, and the little boy moves to another town where the teacher smiles and says that painting should be fun; the little boy, however, paints flowers in neat rows of green and red, and when the teacher asks him why, he explains that flowers are red and leaves are green and that is the only way to see them! Sharing this story with teachers allowed them to keep in mind the impact they have on the lives of students. We shared the same message with school leaders, but to emphasize their impact on staff rather than on students. Embrace your staff, encourage your staff, and allow your staff to see all the colors of the rainbow, but do not cut off their ideas or their thoughts—remember, they are teaching the students, not you.

We also often shared Haim Ginott's saying about the teacher (see Appendix III) as his message, echoing Chapin's, is something you as a leader should remind your staff but more importantly yourself of as you set about supporting and responding to your staff. Throughout our writing, we have referred to students as having special needs, disabilities, and handicaps, and once we began asking ourselves which is the most appropriate designation, we realized that *special needs* came from Chapter 766, *disabled* came from PL 94-142, and *handicapped* came from the Education for All Handicapped Children Act. We think that all students have special needs, and we have also come to recognize that *disabled* sends a negative message about the student and *handicapped* points to something standing in the student's way. While we're not sure when or where *differently abled* originated, this term, to our thinking, sends a clearer picture of the students with whom we have had the great pleasure of working throughout our careers. All children have abilities; some just have different abilities than others, and we must recognize these differences as part of being a child regardless of age, height, weight, eye color, hair length, skin color, family background, socioeconomic status, zip code, or any other characteristics.

As the educational leaders for the provision of special education services to students with special needs, we must be aware of and appreciate the differences and similarities among our students. Yes, some students will have different abilities than their peers, but our experiences have given us the opportunity to see a student with hearing loss assist a typical classmate and a student with Down syndrome support a student in a wheelchair. Regardless of the identified disability, each student possesses an individual set of abilities, which may not match what "we" expect but are abilities just the same. The laws have had a significant impact on students, both in special education and in general education. One of our own children came home from school one day in the third grade, in tears, and when asked what was wrong, she lamented that a classmate was not allowed on stage to prepare for the Memorial Day presentation. Upon further investigation, it was determined that this student had cerebral palsy and used a wheelchair. He had his own assistant and a communication device that allowed him to communicate with the teacher and his classmates; to our child, however, he was just another student in the classroom and belonged on stage with the group. Turns out, she would go on to become a special education teacher, and this classmate may just have been the deciding factor. And so, having stated our beliefs based on our personal and professional values, we embark on this effort to provide a practical guide to becoming an effective ASE. You, too, will be responsible for providing a FAPE in the LRE, but access to an education is not enough. The quality of instruction must be held to the highest standard, and must be socially just, to ensure that students with special needs make effective progress toward meeting those high standards and expand on their abilities.

Have good intentions gone awry? Both Freedman (2017) and Moscovitch (1993) refer to this question. In Chapter 1, we referenced President Ford's concern prior to the implementation of PL 94-142 regarding the potential unintended burdens the law contained. The law was also intended to reimburse states for 40% of their annual special education expenditures, but that never materialized. In fact, the federal reimbursement has never even reached 20%. Those of us who have worked with the law(s) and witnessed their impact on the lives of students see good intentions achieved, and while difference and debate regarding costs, small student-to-teacher ratios, paperwork demands, and so on will continue, we have always focused on the needs of students, developing programs to allow students to remain in the LRE, and the provision of quality services and instruction. As we have said for all these years, focusing on the needs of the students will never steer you wrong or set your intentions off-track.

CHAPTER SUMMARY

Establishing a clearly stated belief system that is formulated from your own personal and professional values is essential to identifying your priorities both toward the position of ASE and toward students with special needs. To succeed over the long term, you must realize, as you gain experiences, the need to review and update your belief system to correspond to new evidence-based practices, areas where you have not been successful, and how your continued experience has informed your thinking. This willingness to adjust, modify, and expand your thinking about your beliefs will demonstrate that you are a leader willing to make change for the benefit of students. Always remind yourself that your staff as well as your students' parents are looking to you for leadership. Your job is to ensure that identified students receive the services they require—not more, not less. How you share your beliefs and expectations will set the course for the culture of your department. Once again, it is important to remember that it takes time (three to five years) to change a culture, and holding steady to your beliefs and expectations will establish that culture accordingly.

3

Your Role as Administrator of Special Education

Have you asked yourself why you aspire to be an administrator of special education (ASE) or, if you are already in the position, why you took the job? Do you want better pay, more authority, a step toward becoming a superintendent or assistant superintendent, or all of the above? Or, do you want to make a difference in the lives of students and parents or staff? It is important to reflect on these questions as you take on the daunting task of administering a special education department; after all, you will be not only the leader but also the manager of your department. As noted in Chapter 2, your beliefs and values must always drive your decision making and the direction of your department.

Leadership and Management

Several colleagues of ours were known to overmanage and could never separate their role as a manager from their role as a leader. Leadership and management are not the same thing. While they are complementary, they differ in several important ways.

Leadership is about vision and innovation; it involves envisioning the program structure as well as how to disseminate and incorporate your beliefs and expectations throughout your district.

Management, on the other hand, involves maintaining the standard of excellence you espouse to. Still another way to look at leadership and management is that a leader innovates, and a manager administrates the innovation.

It is important to remember that you are the face of special education in your district, and often the message you need to send is not a popular one. You may be informing a principal or staff member why they cannot do something the way they had wanted to; explaining to a parent that the district was not responsible for providing a specific service or assessment; or even informing your superintendent of a new legal mandate, a regulation change, a new out-of-district placement, or another requirement that they may not want to hear.

One former colleague attended a retirement party and sat next to his former superintendent, who said to him, "I owe you an apology." "What do you mean?" our colleague asked, and the superintendent admitted that when our colleague came into his office, he never saw the person; he saw a green book—the regulations appeared in green at that time—and he knew he was about to be presented with a difficult scenario or new requirement that would cost a lot of money.

We have mentioned the ASE as being known as a "professional flack catcher," and how difficult that role can be. Anyone in the community not pleased with some aspect of special education will visualize, and blame, you.

School Committee

On the occasion that you must deliver a presentation to your school committee, keep a few pointers in mind and always be prepared for surprises. You may be presenting on a specific topic; however, you have a captive audience, and committee members might raise an issue or concern they have been thinking about and ask for your reaction. For the many school committee presentations we made, the obvious goal was to be comprehensive and to never have a committee member asking for more. In preparation, we would go through all our difficult cases, budget items, building issues, state directives, and on and on, reminding ourselves that any topic would be fair game once we had concluded our discussion of the primary topic. We always rehearsed our presentation or a specific response prior to any school committee meeting. If you are required to attend all school committee meetings and you are not presenting, prepare yourself anyway; in our experience, on many occasions presenters would call upon us to address an issue or answer a question that grew out of an ongoing discussion. If you find yourself unable to respond, don't hesitate to indicate the need for follow-up and assure the individual committee member, or the whole committee if need be, that you'll get back to them in a timely manner.

State Department of Education

A valuable source of information, your state department of education (DOE) oversees how your district is complying with the law. In our experience, when the state DOE conducts a compliance review, it is to see if the district has "crossed all the *t*s and dotted all the *i*s," not to assess the quality of your programs or the quality of the instruction you provide to students. State DOE officials enter your district with the intention of determining if your district has met all timelines, translated all documents, conducted three-year reevaluations, and so on, and if not, to determine your action plan and timeline. You will never hear your state DOE asking you to have staff trained in the Wilson Reading System, the Orton-Gillingham Approach, Lindamood Phoneme Sequencing (LiPS), or Fundations, for example. We always defaulted to giving the department as little as possible, and if they required more, they never failed to let us know. We also refrained from asking questions of the state DOE as we saw many of our colleagues receive answers they were not prepared to hear. Rather, we believed in doing what needed to be done, as we saw fit. If at some point your state DOE does not approve of your approach, they will tell you and allow you to make a change.

Assuming the Position

As you take on this job, many aspects can and likely will be daunting, as mentioned. You may enter a district where the same person led the department for many years, and everyone is looking to you for change. Be leery of the staff who come to your door in the early days with advice. Personnel matters may need to be addressed, but be patient. Starting in your office, look at how staff members communicate, how they handle the mail, how they answer phone calls, and so on; simply put, observe and absorb. We discussed leadership styles earlier, and if your style differs from your predecessor's, you will need to establish your expectations for and with your staff. You may inherit staff members who do their own thing and have become accustomed to having it their way. Again, be patient and observe in order to develop how you want to conduct the difficult conversation, and remember to always conduct these conversations behind a closed door. You may see the union get involved early on as you go about establishing your expectations.

In fact, you may find it productive to seek out the union leadership to introduce yourself and let them know that, although you are not predicting as much, staff may not accept your expectations and may choose to seek union assistance. Assure the union leaders that if you see that as a possibility, you will let them know, as no one likes to be blindsided. We have said for years that the students are rarely the problem; it is generally the adults. Your job is to provide these adults, be it staff or parents, with the training and knowledge they require and, as stated earlier, when difficulties arise, to go behind a closed door to address the issue.

Trust Your Instincts

You know more than you give yourself credit for. When we took on the job of ASE, the Massachusetts law (Chapter 766) was just being implemented, and we had very few places to turn for advice. We found ourselves "trusting our gut" on many major decisions related to the law and the governing regulations. Now, 47 years later, multiple resources are available to turn to for assistance and advice, but you still may need to rely on your gut.

CHAPTER SUMMARY

You will be given a job description when you apply for the ASE position, and it is highly likely that you will revise it after three months, six months, or one year. The role you have assumed or are currently maintaining is the most difficult position in the school district, even more difficult than the superintendent. Some may dispute that statement, but we believe that we are on sound footing when we say your role is to be everything to everyone. Most importantly, your role is to design systems within your

(Continued)

district that simplify the work needed to identify and service students with special needs and to identify the areas that cause you pain along with developing strategies to alleviate that pain.

Whether you're dealing with one issue or several, to achieve success you must construct strategies that assist you in effectively addressing those issues with a positive attitude and approach. It is not easy, but to succeed you need to have control of your day, your schedule, the issues, and your purpose for being in this position. As noted, throughout our careers we have had the opportunity to work with many new ASEs and listen to their concerns about the job.

We often heard, for example, that they received no internal training when they began in the position, and this meant that people assumed that they, as ASEs, knew what to do. We understand it can take years to fully comprehend the innuendoes of the school district, however, and having to fend for yourself is not very comforting. Often you are not even aware of the question to ask until you are faced with it, and while figuring out where to go for an answer can be very time-consuming, once you do find out whom to ask their response is usually positive and they are usually very willing to assist.

So where do you go if the district has not oriented you to the significant areas of concern and the go-to knowledge worker for each area? If your secretary has been in the district a while, it is highly likely they can be of great assistance. Many new ASEs struggle with establishing a relation-ship with their secretary and how they can help. Start early, assisting your secretary with your expectations, and keep in mind that you may have different expectations for your secretary than your predecessor did. Remember that it takes 25 to 30 repetitions for a task to become part of a person's routine.

If you lose of sight of why you accepted or are working toward the ASE position, it is time for a career change. As we noted earlier, ASEs are professional flack catchers, and you likely will get little recognition for the work you do and the hours you devote to your job. On the other hand, the work can be incredibly positive and enormously effective. When you take the time to identify all areas of responsibility in your position and put in place the organizational strategies, systems, and procedures required, you will find yourself in a position to reflect on the benefits for students, staff, your department, and your school district.

Confidentiality 4

We briefly mentioned confidentiality in Chapter 3. Now, let's dedicate some specific time to confidentiality—a mainstay of everything that administrators of special education (ASEs) oversee. Our state, Massachusetts, requires ASEs to review with all staff their responsibilities in terms of confidential information. We would follow up this discussion with a memorandum (see Appendix IV) and revisit its content throughout the school year. Primarily, we advised our staff to ask themselves, if sensitive information concerned their child or a member of their family, how they would want it to be maintained or shared. You and your staff are privy to a great deal of information on students and their families. Beyond educational information, you may have psychological assessment results, home assessment information, hospital placement information, independent evaluation results, information from your state's department of social services or department of children and family services, and much more. Ensuring that everyone understands your expectations for maintaining confidential information is one of your primary roles as the ASE. We adhere to the old adage that offices have doors for a reason. When you need to discuss a family or personnel issue, bring the discussion into your office (or a private space in a school) and close the door; other than the individuals involved, no one needs to hear what you wish to discuss. In addition, after the meeting, remind the individuals present of the need for—and the expectation that they will adhere to—confidentiality.

We found ourselves in numerous situations over our careers where a staff member, from either general or special education, shared student information inappropriately. In one situation, a staff member felt the need to share a personal family story with anyone within earshot, a distraction brought to our attention after it had occurred a few times. We invited the individual into the office to explain our concern, but also to convey that we understood the importance of the story to the person who had overshared. We informed this staff member that if they ever needed to tell a personal story at work, they could come into the office, close the door, and share; we further explained, however, that if we ever heard such a story had been shared outside of the office again, it would result in administrative follow-up.

Another time, a staff member said to a parent, off the record, "I think your child belongs in a special education private day program." This staff member had been providing direct special education services to the student, in a public school, and the case was scheduled to go to hearing as a rejected Individualized Education Plan (IEP). Well, when the attorney for the district heard this comment, he advised we settle with the parent; otherwise, the parent would prevail—meaning the parent's attorney would call the district's special education teacher as the first witness at the hearing.

In yet another situation, one of us observed a general education teacher going through a student's file. When approached and questioned, the teacher indicated that they needed information on a student they had taught the previous school year, and was immediately advised that teachers only had the right to access information on current students. This incident led to the development of a procedure for all staff when accessing a student file and a meeting with all district administrators to inform them of the procedure and review regulations related to the confidentiality of student records. Our state regulates how to handle student records, and the regulations incorporate all the requirements of the Family Educational Rights and Privacy Act (FERPA), the federal law related to student records. We have found that most staff and school leaders are not aware of the requirements of these regulations, and as stated earlier, rather than leave each school to address them in their own way, all schools within the district must handle access to student records in the same manner.

Confidentiality, whether in a small, medium, or large district, will always be a touch point for you as an ASE. All district staff must understand the importance of keeping information about students and their families confidential, available only to those who need to know because they work directly with the student. It is essential that you put in place clear policies and practices that will protect both student and family information. Trust is a delicate aspect of your work as well as the work of district staff. Building trust takes time, and a one-time breach of confidentiality may be all it takes for you to lose that trust permanently.

CHAPTER SUMMARY

Know and share with all school personnel, including all building administrators, your requirements regarding student confidentiality, and be sure to inform school-based staff, in writing, of their role with respect to student confidentiality, student files, and general or specific information. Not maintaining confidentiality in terms of information about a student or their family can come around to bite you and your district on the back side. Outlining the rules, requirements, and procedures regarding confidentiality for all students and their families is clearly important, but all too often districts do not give enough credence to the issue. As repeatedly indicated, confidentiality is a top priority, and how you share student information requires protection. We will also address confidentiality related to due process proceedings in Chapter 22.

5

Section 504 of the Rehabilitation Act of 1973

When the Rehabilitation Act of 1973, a landmark civil rights law, was passed, Section 504 of the act prohibited discrimination based on disability. Although you may not have any responsibilities related to Section 504, we know several school districts where the administrator of special education (ASE) oversees this process. If you hold the position of assistant superintendent of student services or administrator of pupil personnel services, your duties may include Section 504 as well. Should you be charged with overseeing Section 504, you will focus on bringing clarity to the process of decision making for qualified students.

Referred to for many years as the "barrier-free access law" because it initially dealt with access to services, Section 504 is a civil rights statute that requires the needs of students with disabilities to be met as adequately as the needs of their peers without disabilities. One district in our state of Massachusetts developed a brochure (Bragar et al., 1979) to inform other districts how to go about providing access for students with limited mobility to a classroom located on the second floor of a school, for example, or how to make educational services available to a student in a wheelchair when the school is not equipped with a ramp. Section 504 always contained inclusive language: "No otherwise qualified individual with a disability in the United States, as defined in section 706(8) of this title, shall, solely by reason of her or his disability, be excluded from the participation in, be denied the benefits of, or be subjected to discrimination under any program or activity receiving Federal financial assistance" [29 U.S.C. §794(a), 34 C.F.R. §104.4(a)]; however, not until the passing of the Individuals With Disabilities Education Act (IDEA) did this language take on any real significance. Eligibility for services under Section 504 is extended to "any person who: (i) has a mental or physical impairment that substantially limits one or more major life activity; (ii) has a record of such an impairment; or (iii) is regarded as having such an impairment" [34 C.F.R. §104.3(j)(1)]. Similar to the definition of effective progress in general education, under special education law and Section 504 in particular the term *substantial limitation* has been debated , but major life activities include self-care, manual tasks, walking, seeing, speaking, sitting, thinking, learning, breathing, concentrating, interacting with others, and working.

The Americans With Disabilities Act Amendments Act (ADAAA), effective January 1, 2009, expanded the list of major life activities to include reading, concentrating, standing, lifting, bending, and more to provide for individuals with attention deficit hyperactivity disorder (ADHD), dyslexia, cancer, diabetes, severe allergies, chronic asthma, Tourette syndrome, digestive disorders, cardiovascular disorders, depression, conduct disorder, oppositional defiant disorder, HIV/AIDS, behavior disorders, and temporary disabilities such as a broken writing arm or a broken leg. The law also covers conditions that are episodic or in remission, such as juvenile arthritis, if when active they substantially limit one or more major life activities for the student. It is important to note, however, that Section 504 excludes students who currently use illegal drugs or alcohol.

While the term *substantial limitation* is not defined in the federal regulations, according to a letter from the Office for Civil Rights (OCR), "this is a determination to be made by each local school district and depends on the nature and severity of the person's disabling condition." In terms of substantial limitations, students must be measured against their same-age peers who do not have disabilities in the general population and without benefit of medication or other mitigating measures such as learned behavioral or adaptive neurological modifications, assistive technology, or accommodations. Unlike special education, the federal regulations for Section 504 do not require or even mention parent participation in the decision making involving the child. Parents must always, however, not only be notified before their child is evaluated and/or placed under Section 504, but also be given a copy of the child's Section 504 accommodation plan if the committee determines that the child qualifies for services under Section 504. Whether or not to include parents on the decision-making committee must be determined by each school district and be spelled out in the district's procedures for implementing Section 504. Involving parents is considered a best practice but, as noted, not a requirement. The regulations governing Section 504 indicate that "placement decisions are to be made by a group of persons who are knowledgeable about the child, the meaning of the evaluation data, placement options, least restrictive environment requirements, and comparable facilities."

Unlike the special education process, which requires adhering to various timelines, 504 plans do not specify timelines in either federal or state law. Many school districts follow guidelines and often keep to the same timelines as specified for Individualized Education Plans (IEPs). No testing is required, and the district must depend on all data available including the student's grades over the past few years. When a student is determined to have a disability that significantly limits a major life activity, the Team then develops a 504 plan to incorporate the accommodations required for the student to progress. Section 504 is considered civil rights law, and parents can bring suit against a school district when they believe that their child's civil rights have been denied. Similar to the 1993 *Doe v. Withers* case in West Virginia, in all of the cases on which we have consulted, all of the parties involved were initially cited but, as the investigation developed, some of the citations were eliminated. Although the student in *Withers* had an IEP, the parents chose to file a civil rights complaint. You can imagine the anxiety and stress placed on anyone involved in such a case. As you may recall from Chapter 1, Mr. Withers was a general education teacher who refused to implement the accommodations for a student, but he was not the only one. The school committee, superintendent, and ASE were all originally cited and later removed once it became clear that they had made efforts to work with Mr. Withers to follow the accommodations. One of the cases we were involved in cited the actions by a building principal, school psychologist, and adjustment counselor, and it took many months working with the Office of Special Education Programs (OSEP) and our school attorney to resolve the matter.

CHAPTER SUMMARY

As noted, whether or not you have Section 504 responsibilities in your district, your staff should know their role when a student is found ineligible for special education services. It is important to keep special education and Section 504 on parallel but separate tracks, and developing a clear understanding of a substantial limitation to a major life activity is critical to the process. As indicated in the West Virginia case, a Section 504 complaint may ultimately be handled by OSEP and the OCR. In Massachusetts, complaints may be resolved internally, within the district, or through the district's appeal process, or be forwarded to the Bureau of Special Education Appeals (BSEA), which would hear the case in the same way as a special education IEP disagreement. Your state may work with yet another due process procedure, and we encourage you to become familiar with the process.

PART II

Program and Service Delivery Considerations

6 Procedural Manual

The need became very evident to us, after a short period of time as administrators of special education (ASEs), for staff throughout the district to receive the required information to ensure consistent practice by all school-based personnel. A procedural manual, now mandated by most regulations at the state level, must be in place to provide all staff with the written guidance to function within a highly regulated environment with respect to the requirements and procedural safeguards for protecting the rights of children and parents. Sound documentation of procedures makes everyone's job (and decision making) easier. It also elimininates surprises, and no one likes to be blindsided—not your students, not parents, not colleagues, and certainly not yourself.

In a procedural manual, all aspects of operational practice based on regulations are presented in written format to ensure that *all* school-based personnel know what to do on the job. Staff can refer to the manual to determine who is responsible for certain steps and actions, and what is expected of all school-based staff involved with the processes of referral, evaluation, eligibility determination, Individualized Education Plan (IEP) development, service delivery, annual review, and reevaluation. Having this form of written documentation in everyone's hands is crucial for the district to reduce the potential for miscommunication and missteps by school-based staff as well as those responsible for direct service to students with disabilities.

Paperwork is a necessary evil of special education. We indicated in Chapter 1 President Gerald Ford's concerns about the potential for excessive paperwork when the federal law was passed in 1975, and clearly they have proven true. Among the requirements in recent years that add to the paperwork are the many forms needed to justify referring a student for a learning disability, transitional planning, bullying, restraint, and so on. A system of protocols and procedures must be established to assist all staff involved, but more importantly to put in place safeguards to ensure their actions protect the rights of students and parents.

Your responsibilities as an ASE involve ensuring that the district complies with all aspects of the law and the regulations governing the law. As one of our previous superintendents was known to say, we were not a system of schools; we were a school system. In developing procedures for your department, remind yourself that everyone needs to adhere to the same expectations in the same "systemic" way. Consistent practice by all staff within the department will lead to smoother function of all services by all providers regardless of the size of the district. "Screw-ups" will occur, but with a well-thought-out and well-documented procedural manual, they will be few and far between during your tenure.

The procedural manual should include regulatory steps, sample forms, and actions intended for involved individuals at all levels of the referral, evaluation, and eligibility determination process along with the development, implementation, and follow-up of the IEP after establishing a student's eligibility for special education services. According to our experience, a comprehensive manual should contain an established mission or vision statement for the department as well as an established chain of command that allows all staff to understand where and how to find answers to various questions. The mission or vision statement sets the course for your department, and the chain of command simplifies how staff navigate the complexities of the special education process from beginning to end. Including a glossary of terms and definitions will also give staff a clear, consistent, and comprehensive understanding of the various special education procedures. In addition, including a "Frequently Asked Questions" section will give staff, district administrators, and others the opportunity to find quick solutions to some frequent problems as well as to locate procedural requirements. Other essential content includes the following:

- A statement on the district's perspective toward special education.
- General education classroom interventions.
- The Teacher Assistance Team process (such as for a Child Study Team or a general education initiative).
- The referral process.
- The evaluation process.
    - Description of the process.
    - Team members' roles and responsibilities.
    - Eligibility guidelines.
    - A description of an actual Team meeting process (i.e., how to conduct such a meeting).
    - Extended evaluation.
    - Independent evaluation.[1]
    - Rejected IEP process.
    - Emergency evaluation.
    - Crisis intervention services.
    - Determination of ineligibility for services.
    - Regular Education Service Plan (RESP) or Section 504 plan.
- Sample IEP in full detail.
- Transition planning from one level to the next.
- Tutorial instructional services for home, school, and hospital.
- Home-based services.
- Progress reports.
- Annual review and reevaluation.
- Transition to adult services.
- Special education questions and answers.
- Assessment and testing guidelines and practices.
- Samples of required operational forms.
- Transportation practices.
- Discipline of students with IEPs.
- Physical restraint policies and practices.

---

[1] Independent evaluations are part of the regulations and an area of focus particularly due to the timelines to meet and the process to follow to determine financial responsibility.

- IEP checklist.
- Special education resources at the local, state, and national level.

A later addition to the list of procedures is significant disproportionality, a focus of the Individuals With Disabilities Education Act (IDEA) in recent years. States are, annually, expected to track all eligible students identified as having a physical disability, an intellectual disability, a specific learning disability, an emotional disability (disturbance), speech or language impairments, other health impairments, and autism. Students with disabilities ages 6 through 21 or 22 placed in general education classrooms for less than 40% of their school day, as well as in separate and residential schools, or removed through disciplinary action are also tracked. This includes out-of-school suspensions and expulsions of 10 or fewer days, out-of-school suspensions and expulsions for 10 or more days, in-school suspensions of 10 or fewer days, and in-school suspensions of 10 or more days, as well as total removal from school through a disciplinary action. Your state must calculate the rates of identification, placement, and disciplinary removal in the aforementioned categories for seven racial or ethnic groups (Black, Native American or Alaska Native, Asian, Hispanic or Latino, Hawaiian Native or Pacific Islander, multiracial, and white) and compare them to the rates for all other children within your district. Because this area of compliance can sneak up on you if you're not careful, you and your staff must be mindful of these data.

This list of components may appear extensive and a bit overwhelming. We have learned, however, that putting in place such an extensive document and providing training will allow you to avoid many mistakes and errors and, most importantly, a procedural handbook stops paperwork and student cases from falling through the cracks. As an administrator, you need to establish processes that you want for your district so that all school-based personnel understand and comply with your expectations, each other's roles and responsibilities, and their own roles. You will need to ensure each of the content components indicated earlier are written in a way that gives staff a clear understanding.

Whenever we put in place a list of procedures for the staff to work from, we kept in mind the idea of "paint by numbers," reminding ourselves that the manual needed to be clearly written and not cumbersome to understand. Staff have a difficult job, and making tasks more complex than necessary is not productive. Instead, keep tasks as simple as possible while always striving to achieve the expected outcome. You will, of course, need to periodically review and update the procedural manual as new federal and state regulations and requirements come into existence. In addition, during your tenure you will probably realize that some practices and procedures need revising to ensure effective operations.

In concert with the procedural manual, you will need to fully understand the procedural safeguards that must be in place. One significant aspect of the ASE position is to ensure district compliance with state and federal special education law. The federal law requires that states monitor local district compliance, and to that end states have established audit and review processes, so if your district's special education procedural manual is available to all staff and understood by all constituents, you are ahead of the curve. If your district does not provide access to the procedural manual and safeguards, then you and your department staff need to make it a priority and primary focus.

Compliance Factors

Generally, your state will look for compliance with timelines, notices, forms, parental complaints, disciplining of special education students, and other data collected through various reports. This process has seen many variations; for example, our state, Massachusetts, began with full-audit Teams including parents, state agency representatives, and district officials visiting school districts for a comprehensive look at all compliance related to special education. The state then turned to a so-called desk audit where the local district submitted requested information and the state followed up only upon determination of a need for compliance. Next came compliance reviews, both full (every 6 years) and mid (every 3 years), where again the local district and a small Team of state personnel conducted the bulk of the work, before visiting the district to confirm the accuracy of the data. Currently, the our state is conducting "Tiered Focused Monitoring," or determining risk assessment based on the accountability level of the district along with the following risk factors:

- Special education disproportionality data.
- Identification.
- Discipline.
- Problem resolution system.

- Compliance data.
- Public school monitoring report data.

Compliance is a major focus of your job. If you uncover areas of noncompliance, you and your district will be required to submit an action plan indicating steps the district will take to achieve compliance. This process can be very time-consuming and potentially costly to the district and your budget.

One of us found out early on that sometimes you need to take a stand to protect and ensure services for students with IEPs. We received a call from a staff member informing us that their principal was using special education staff as substitutes to cover general education classes. Obviously, when this occurs, students miss their required services. Before we responded, however, we wanted to verify if the same thing was taking place in other schools. The inquiry had to be discreet so as not to throw any staff members under the proverbial bus. It turned out that this practice occurred in virtually every school, so we drafted and sent a memorandum to every principal in the district, informing them that special education staff were *never* to be used as substitutes. At the following week's administrator's meeting, the superintendent slid a copy of the memo across the table and asked, "What is this?" He was informed that it was my responsibility to ensure that IEPs were followed and that the school district was not put in a compromising position (noncompliance) by failing to provide students with the services required in their IEP. The superintendent then continued on with the meeting. Needless to say, taking this position certainly tested the relationship with many principals; however, we believed that our job *was* to protect not only the services for each student with an IEP but also the overall integrity of the staff within the special education department—*our* department. The overall message to the principals and other administrators was "Don't shoot the messenger; the law is the law."

The last comprehensive review of special education in our state, conducted by Dr. Thomas Hehir and colleagues, occurred in 2012. We thought sharing some outcomes from the report might allow you to reflect on how your district addresses these areas. Hehir and his Team drew several conclusions from their work, which began with Massachusetts having the second-highest number of students identified with disabilities in the United States (17+%). Additional statistics indicated that approximately 23% of low-income students in Massachusetts have disabilities, compared to about 15% of students who are not low-income. Additionally, Spanish-speaking students account for approximately 55% of all Massachusetts Limited English Proficient (LEP) students, but they represent approximately 75% of LEP students eligible for special education services. In referencing inclusive efforts throughout the state, Hehir indicated that students with "high-incidence" disabilities who spent more of their time in mainstream settings tended to score higher on statewide tests than students with "high-incidence" disabilities who spent less of their time with typically developing peers. He also indicated that in our state 63 of 100 students receiving a special education spend at least 80% of their day in classrooms with typical peers, and that the likelihood of a student being integrated into general education classes might be malleable and influenced by district policies. The variability between districts regarding inclusion rates suggests that room is available to influence inclusion rates via district-level policies. Your state may have criteria for determining full and partial inclusion. Our state, for example, indicates how to determine partial and full inclusion as part of a student's IEP placement. Full inclusion is defined as special education services outside the general education classroom less than 21% of the time. Partial inclusion is defined as special education services outside the general education classroom 21% to 60% of the time. Students who receive special education services outside the general education classroom more than 60% of the school day are considered to be in a substantially separate classroom or placement.

Hehir and colleagues (2012) noted that rates of identification vary *substantially* from district to district. In some districts, more than 3 in 10 students with disabilities receive services in *substantially separate settings* (spending between 0% and 40% of their days with typically developing peers), while in other districts this figure is less than 1 in 10. Further, Black and Hispanic or Latino students with disabilities are educated in substantially separate settings at higher rates than white and Asian students with disabilities in middle and high schools. All of these data can provide significant assistance to your district when determining what works well and where to address some areas of concern over time.

Monthly Activity Guide

Along with the procedural manual, you need to create a monthly activity guide. This guide can begin in September, but must outline by each week of the month what activities, department- or district-wise, your office is expected to complete. Child find activities, budget development, census reporting, preschool screening, notifications to staff and parents, self-reminders to complete and submit district or state reports, staff caseload reports, articles of information for the local newspaper, high-stakes testing timelines, alternative assessment timelines and requirements, summer school dates, timelines for referrals, who is eligible, transition activities, and more—no matter the procedure, this guide should act as a reminder for you so that during the hectic school year you do not forget what is due, when it is due, and if others by position need to assist in gathering data for your reports. Setting up this monthly or weekly guide can greatly assist in ensuring the smooth operation of your office and department. Some weeks may have numerous tasks, while others may have only one or two along with your daily routine. This guide will help you prevent the occasional misstep; if established in your school's Google or Microsoft Office 365 Calendar as an automatic reminder, you'll never again forget to complete a task.

Department Staff Decorum at Team Meetings

As ASEs, we spent a great deal of time on how staff understood their role at Team meetings. Remembering that most people need to do something 25 to 30 times before it becomes routine, we knew that setting expectations could not be a one-off; we needed to keep it in the forefront. We expected everyone to share their findings and knowledge of the student and that no one would speak for someone else. This meant that we did not want the speech therapist making recommendations for the occupational therapist, for example, or the special education teacher making recommendations for the school psychologist. We expected a Team approach and that the meeting chairperson would take responsibility for directing everyone toward the common goal(s). In Massachusetts, the initial regulations referred to Team meetings as core Evaluation Team meetings, and in fact many continue to describe students as referred for a "core"; in some respects, the assessment process is like putting students under a microscope and looking into the core of their learning abilities. The process of several professionals assessing a student in several areas lends itself to the Team feeling like they must find something, as someone believes the referred student is not learning and therefore must have a learning difficulty or disability. When the Team determines that a student is not eligible for special education services, certain interested parties—either the staff member who made the referral or the parent—will likely not be pleased. Team members also know that they need to function in the school, and without any efforts put forward prior to the referral (prereferral), they are sending the student back to the referring party without any assistance. As stated earlier, this often leads to determining a student's eligibility simply because members of the Team feel guilty that there's no other way to assist this student than special education, often the only game in town.

CHAPTER SUMMARY

In focusing on strategies that can assist you in the ASE role, the procedural manual, an activity guide, and decorum at Team meetings are vehicles for you and your staff to institute effective practices within your department and the district. You and all school-based staff need to know how the department functions and operates so that you do not have to spend substantial time backpedaling for missteps. All district staff (administrators, general and special education) need to understand the operating practices of the district with respect to compliance issues and regulatory requirements. These proven strategies not only assist you in your role but will assist the school-based staff in their roles as well. We never wanted to hear "that's how they do it at the other school." Keep reminding yourself that it is a school system and not a system of schools. The more consistency your schools have, the clearer everyone will be on the requirements for addressing matters as they arise in a unified way.

Process, Procedures, Practices

Referral, Evaluation, and Determination of Eligibility for Specialized Instruction

7

The new laws, Chapter 766 (the Bartley-Daly Act) and PL 94-142 (the Education for All Handicapped Children Act), changed the paradigm of education in the state of Massachusetts and throughout the country. Administrators of special education (ASEs) now had Child Find, prereferral and referral requirements, timelines to meet, assessments to conduct (within specified time limits), parent notifications to make, Evaluation Team meetings to conduct, parents' rights to share, confidentiality to hold, Individualized Education Plans (IEPs) to write, programs with options and choices to develop, and services to render, among many other steps. School districts very apparently needed to develop procedures to fulfill these requirements, including training for staff, both special and general educators, and especially school administrators. The new special education laws meant that regular education teachers would play a significant role in servicing the needs of eligible students. As we mentioned in the introduction to this book, "when a paradigm shifts, everyone goes back to zero" (Barker, 1989), and the new laws returned all teachers to zero understanding of their role in decision making and service provision to identified students.

COVID-19, too, has seen general and special educators starting at zero understanding of how to provide virtual as well as safe in-person instruction to all students.

ASEs must not lose sight of Child Find responsibilities. The Child Find mandate, part of the Individuals With Disabilities Education Act (IDEA), requires public school districts to identify, locate, and evaluate all children with disabilities from birth through the age of 21 or 22. Under the federal law, public schools must look for, find, and evaluate children who need special education services, including those who are homeschooled, in private schools, migrants, or without homes. Be aware that your state may have additional Child Find requirements.

Should your district contain a private or parochial school, you will also be responsible for calculating, and making available to the private school, the proportional share of your federal entitlement funds. Although you are only responsible for the IEPs of students who reside in your district, the IEPs of other students in attendance will be handled by the district where the student resides. The federal law requires proportional share for private and parochial schools, and you must be aware of the responsibilities required by your state.

In the early days of the new laws, students, once identified as eligible, would receive their services outside of the general education classroom, which meant coordinating schedules with their teachers to ensure they missed general education classroom instruction in only those content areas where they needed special education assistance. This required the development of basic procedures, and from our standpoint, there were many. The prereferral requirement, for example, played out in the regulations that governed the law. School personnel were required to make efforts to provide alternative service approaches (Regular Education Initiative) to students potentially in need of services within the general education classroom by general educators. Prereferral is a basic procedure but for the most part out of the ASE's control. We have observed many school districts with no solid prereferral process in place, no tiered levels of instruction for general education to utilize, and little if any training on differentiated instruction.

For numerous districts, the prereferral process is not practiced with consistency and fidelity at every school. Many districts also fail to provide tiered levels of instruction for general educators. Inevitably, in our experience, this leads to providing services, as indicated in Chapter 6, "out of guilt." All members of the student's Team must understand that they are "the only game in town" regarding the provision of services in a different way for the student. This often starts with determining the student's eligibility to ensure receipt of services. When we examine this aspect further, we encounter many conflicting dynamics within the referral, assessment, and Team process.

Once the parent gives permission to assess, the student is tested for academic, psychological, and other areas of performance to determine the student's ability to make effective progress, and those conducting the tests then spend a substantial amount of time determining if the student has a disability that interferes with their ability to make effective progress in line with their peers in general education. Some have compared this to looking under a microscope. When the assessors and teachers realize that the district has no other service capacity option but special education, everyone begins to focus on that instead of ways to assist the student with remaining fully in general education. Administrators in your district must take steps to familiarize all staff with your state department of education inclusion practices, principles of Universal Design for Learning (UDL), Positive Behavioral Interventions and Supports (PBIS), differentiated instruction, and social-emotional learning (SEL), among other strategies and interventions intended to equip teachers with the skills necessary to work with diverse learners within their classroom. Schools that train their staff in the utilization of these practices and interventions can consistently, more successfully meet the challenges of their students and gather needed data should a referral to special education be indicated.

Any parent or other caretaker can refer a student, and the school district must honor every referral they receive. The Evaluation Team, including the student's parent(s) or guardian(s) along with all staff who conducted the various student assessments, hears from all the professionals involved as well as the parents, reviews the information on the student, and makes a collective determination on the student's eligibility for special education services. As previously noted, a lack of interventions prior to referral (prereferral/RtI) often leads to significant parent referrals, especially after release of student report cards.

Over the years, efforts have been made to enhance the importance of such activities as set out in the regulations. The Regular Education Initiative of the early 1980s was the first such effort, and Response to Intervention (RtI) the most recent. Both brought good intentions to establish the importance of making efforts for all students before considering special education as an option. Both were also flawed, however, in that no law existed to support their implementation; rather, individual school districts were left to determine their importance and implementation. We have seen, in our role as consultants to school districts, that in districts that currently employ RtI coordinators, these efforts have become a part of the culture. Clearly, though, this is not the norm as we have seen far too many districts with no common RtI or prereferral activities (Child Study Team, Student Assistant Team, Building-Based Assistance Team, Teacher Assistance Team, etc.) in place for students, and if they do engage in prereferral activities, individual school principals or school-based personnel lead the initiative. When the district fails to embrace some form of prereferral, most often the student's parents decide to refer on their own or at the suggestion of building personnel. When this occurs, you as the ASE must assign assessments often without any specific knowledge of the suspected area of disability for the student.

As the ASE, you must be well aware of the timelines established for your state. Many states defer to the federal regulations, Sec. 300.1 to 300.818, regarding the timelines for responding to parents, completing the student assessments, holding the Team meeting, and presenting an IEP for the parents to consider. Appendix VI outlines the requirement in our state that within five working days of the receipt of the referral of a child, the school district shall notify the parents or guardians of such child, in writing and in the primary language of the home, of such referral. Upon receipt of written parental consent, the evaluation process will begin, and within 30 school days the school committee shall provide an evaluation for the student. A Team meeting must be held within 45 days of the initial referral for the student. *All* Team members indicated on the invitation must attend the Team meeting unless the parents grant permission for them not to attend. If the staff member missing the meeting has essential information about the student, they *must* submit a report *in writing* for the Team to consider. Keep in mind that a general education teacher is required to attend Team meetings as well. We are also aware that Team members sometimes indicate that they must leave a meeting, but this *cannot* occur without the permission of the parent. Permission not to attend or to leave a meeting requires parent permission in all instances; as we have stated in Chapters 1 and 6, compliance and procedural requirements must always be at the forefront.

The evaluation shall include an assessment in all areas related to the suspected disability. Over our years as ASEs, we established procedures to ensure consistency in deciding what assessments to conduct.

The regulations explained the potential assessments to consider; however, the question of additional assessments remained, and the more clearly we identified when to include them, the more consistently staff made their decisions. Summaries of all assessments must be completed prior to discussion by the Team, and upon request, summaries shall be made available to the parents at least two days in advance of the Team meeting.

Learning Disabilities: Process and Forms

Learning disabilities likely make up a significant portion of your district's population of students receiving a special education. In recent years, school districts in our state reported that a high percentage (25% on average) of all identified eligible students were considered to have a learning disability. In the early years of the law, eligibility was determined based on a student's ability versus achievement, and although Teams can still consider this factor, they no longer need to consider it as the *only* factor. Ensuring that your staff fully understand the process for making such a determination and the forms required by the Team is essential.

For many years, some considered dyslexia a reading disability while others considered it a learning disability. Most recently, however, it has been referred to as a neurodevelopmental disorder, subcategorized in diagnostic guides as a learning disorder with impairment in reading. Our state identifies dyslexia as a learning disability, and in 2021 the Massachusetts Department of Elementary and Secondary Education released a set of guidelines to assist local districts and parents with their understanding.

In situations where parents disagree with assessments, they may request an independent evaluation, a part of the regulations that requires significant involvement by the ASE. Miriam Kurtzig Freedman wrote about independent evaluations in her 1995 article "The Elevator Theory of Special Education." According to her theory, when parents sought an independent evaluation to determine if their child had a disability that interfered with learning, they would start off with a doctor on the first floor. After hearing from that doctor, if they did not agree with the results, they would get on the elevator and head to the doctor on the second floor. Should they disagree with that doctor, they would ride the elevator to the doctor on the third floor and continue until they received an agreeable diagnosis (clinic shopping). The floor on which the child got off the elevator would determine the diagnosis.

Freedman questions whether students are being encouraged to act like something is wrong to get services, and she points out that learning difficulties may have many roots (that do not connect to an elevator), such as hunger, lack of sleep, living conditions, use of drugs or alcohol, and so on. She further indicates that often labels have replaced motivation and asks, in our rush to do good, have we succeeded?

Independent evaluations are part of the regulations, and an area of focus particularly due to the timelines to meet and the process to follow to determine financial responsibility. In our state, all independent education evaluations must be conducted by qualified persons who are registered, certified, licensed, or otherwise approved. These professionals must also agree to abide by the rates set by the state agency responsible for setting such rates. You will need to determine if your state has a similar agency to set rates related to special education evaluations. On occasion, the unique circumstances of the student may justify a higher individual assessment rate than normally allowed.

Parents may obtain an independent education evaluation at their own expense at any time; however, when a parent requests that the school district provide the funding for an independent education evaluation, the district shall abide by the provisions for a sliding fee scale established by state and federal regulations.

Your district is fully responsible for the costs of an independent evaluation for any student eligible for free or reduced-cost lunch or in the custody of a state agency with an Educational Surrogate Parent appointed in accordance with federal law. The independent educational evaluation must be equivalent to the types of assessments completed by the school district. It is important to note that the district must have provided the assessment to the student; if the district has not conducted an assessment and the parents are requesting one, the district is not responsible unless the parents agree to allow the district to conduct an assessment first.

When you do not know the family's financial status, the sliding fee scale must be utilized, and the family must be given the opportunity to provide income information to determine if they are eligible for public funding of all or part of the costs of an independent education evaluation. Provision of financial information by the family is completely voluntary on their part. The lack of financial information provided by the family will disqualify the family from such additional public funding of all or part of the costs of an independent education evaluation but shall not limit the rights of parents to request public funding. When the parent seeks and receives public funding for an independent education evaluation under these provisions, the parent may request independent assessments in one area, more than one area, or all the areas assessed by the school district. The district is also required to make available to the parent information about the sliding scale in use.

When a family agrees to provide financial information, the district shall consider family size and family income information in relation to federal poverty guidelines. Such information shall include anticipated annual income of the family, including all sources of income and verifying documents. Financial information shall be reviewed by the district, but must be kept confidential during such review, and shall not be copied or maintained in any form at the district except to note that information was provided and reviewed and met or did not meet sliding fee scale standards. Financial documents shall be promptly returned to the parent upon the district's determination of financial income status.

According to the sliding scale, where a family's income is equal to or less than 400% of the federal poverty guidelines, the district shall pay 100% of the costs of an independent education evaluation; where a family's income is between 400% and 500% of the federal poverty guidelines, the district shall pay 75%; where a family's income is between 500% and 600% of the federal poverty guidelines, the district shall pay 50% of the costs of an independent education evaluation; and should the family income exceed 600% of the federal poverty guidelines, the district shall have no obligation to cost-share with the parent.

The school district must reconvene the Team within 10 school days of the school district's receipt of the report of the independent education evaluation. The Team shall consider the independent education evaluation and whether a new or amended IEP is appropriate. Notice we do not say "must accept"; the Team must view the independent evaluation as additional information regarding the student that may or may not require them to change the student's IEP or placement.

The Team meeting consists of the student's parent(s) or guardian(s), the student starting at age 14, all personnel who conducted an assessment, a representative from the district authorized to make decisions, and anyone the parent invites. The student must be identified as having one or more disabilities, and it is important to ensure a consistent procedure for identification with which all staff are familiar. The

13 federal disability categories are demonstrated in the following table. (For the purpose of this chapter, Massachusetts disability category percentages are used as an example from fiscal year 2021.)

DISABILITY CATEGORIES	MASS. %
Autism (added in 1990)	14.30%
Deaf-Blindness	0.10%
Hard of Hearing	0.70%
Emotional Disturbance (Emotional Impairment in Mass.)	9.90%
Developmental Delay (to age 9)	11.60%
Intellectual Disability (ages 10 to 22) (Intellectual Impairment in Mass.)	4.20%
Multiple Disabilities	1.20%
Other Health Impairment	14.40%
Physical Disability	0.50%
Specific Learning Disability	23.70%
Neurological Disabillity	5.50%
Communication Disability	13.60%
Traumatic Brain Injury (added in 1990)	0.025%
Visual Impairment (including blindness)	0.05%

Source: Massachusetts Department of Elementary and Secondary Education Fiscal Year 2021 Census Report.

Students are eligible for services if the Team determines that they have a disability as a result of which they are unable to progress effectively in the general education program without the provision of specially designed instruction (*instruction not normally available to students in general education that is specifically designed for students with this type of disability*) or unable to access the general education curriculum without the provision of one or more related services. If a student is deemed eligible, the Team will write an IEP for the student, containing a profile of the student's strengths and areas of weakness and establishing goals as well as objectives (benchmarks) to assess the student's progress toward achievement of the goals. The IEP may also identify any needed accommodations or modifications that the student requires to make progress and whether the student will require transportation to access their services.

The IEP has gone through several variations over the past 40-plus years, and your state very likely has their own version. In the early days, technology wasn't available, and each IEP was handwritten by teachers and chairpersons. The IEP also utilized carbon-copied paper layers with one copy sent to parents, one provided to teachers, and one for the student's file. In the early 1980s, companies began to develop computerized versions of the IEP, which meant that staff could type information and utilize drop-down menus for goals and objectives specific to the individual student. Today, school districts use data systems that include the IEP, and if they don't, they contract with a company that specializes in the production of IEPs. The old carbon copies were notorious for not copying all the way to the bottom of the page, forcing staff, after all the work of writing the IEP, to deal with a blank copy! This proved particularly true for the old blue school pens, and only after one of us asked our building principal to order black ink pens for three successive years was the mission accomplished. Remember—nothing happens quickly in a bureaucracy!

Once the Team has written an IEP, they must review it annually and reevaluate the student's needs three years after the initial finding and every three years beyond to ensure that the student continues to be eligible to receive specialized instruction and services.

The IEP Team shall ensure that the student's inability to progress results from the disability(ies) and not from a lack of instruction in reading or math, an inability to meet the school discipline code, social maladjustment, or Limited English Proficiency (LEP). Given that the law specifies these as areas in which the Team cannot determine a student eligible, your district should be asking how to determine effective progress, social maladjustment, and lack of instruction in reading or math, as well as an inability to meet the school discipline code. Not answering these questions will leave the Team struggling when the issues come to light at a Team meeting. Further, administrators and staff will draw their own conclusions and make decisions not in line with the intent of the law. At this point, Team members' guilt sometimes plays a role in determining a student's eligibility for special education because no other general education services are available to address the student's needs; hence, as we noted earlier in this chapter, special education is the only game in town.

The Team also identifies the student's specific disability. Again, they must determine the disability based on the results of the assessments conducted by the school personnel. Given these directives, determining effective progress in general education, social maladjustment, and lack of instruction in reading or math, along with an inability to meet the school discipline code, takes on a greater importance. We have found, in our work, that many Teams tend to provide services to a student who may not have a disability, is making progress in general education, and would not require an IEP if general education made accommodations for the child. We have identified this as providing special education services because the Team believes that the only way to ensure that general education provides the needed accommodations (*changes how a student learns the material*) or makes any modifications (*changes what a student is taught or expected to learn*) to the curriculum is to write an IEP for the student. Though we may be stating the obvious, we have seen a similar dynamic in districts and schools that have not implemented a prereferral process, and general education teachers find the only way to access assistance for a student is to advise the parents to write a letter requesting special education services.

Your role is twofold: (1) to discuss student eligibility with your staff and assist them with making decisions when they believe that the student should be served in the general education classroom, and (2) to work with district-wide administration on the importance of interventions prior to the referral of a student to special education. All too often, staff view activities prior to referral as a hoop they need to jump through in order to refer a student for special education. Building principals need to be educated on the importance of prereferral and encouraged to build the process into the culture of their school. The RtI model is essential to a school district's ability to provide regular education intervention and support. We have always believed that if prereferral activities eliminate one student from referral for a special education evaluation, then the efforts have been well worth it.

General education personnel need to know best practices, which include accommodations that assist various learners to perform better in their classrooms and ways to modify and adapt the instruction and expectations when appropriate. As the instructional leaders in their schools, principals should take a lead role in solidifying these efforts long before considering special education referral. In addressing service needs and locations, in general education, everyone must keep in mind that the law requires that students receive a Free and Appropriate Public Education (FAPE), and all services must be provided in the Least Restrictive Environment (LRE). The challenge is to determine when the student can achieve this through general education services and when the student needs a referral for special education services to achieve this goal.

Once the IEP Team has considered all assessment results and determined eligibility based on lack of effective progress, they must begin the process of establishing measurable goals in the areas identified for the student along with measurable objectives to determine progress toward attainment of these goals. The Team must also identify the specialized instruction needed for the student to progress effectively. As previously indicated, *specialized instruction is considered instruction not normally available to students in general education.*

In our state, when the Team does not have conclusive evidence to determine eligibility for a student, they can put in place an extended evaluation, which may last for up to 40 school days. At the conclusion of the extended evaluation, the Team must make a determination of eligibility and placement for the student. An extended evaluation should not be confused with an interim alternative educational setting (IAES) (also known as 45-day placement), which concerns the discipline process under the federal Individuals With Disabilities Education Act (IDEA) and represents a change in placement. Extended evaluations, to the contrary, are not a placement, and a student's participation in an extended evaluation does not constitute a change in placement. Should your state allow for extended evaluations, it is important to find out if "staying put" is attached upon completion of the 40 days.

Parents have the right to disagree with the IEP recommended by the school district. Be aware of two significant things: First, you cannot begin to provide services to a student without the parents' consent. Parents can approve the IEP in full, or they can accept portions of the IEP and reject other parts. Second, if parents reject the IEP presented by the district and the student was already eligible and receiving services, then the "stay put" provision of IDEA comes into play. This means that the student will continue to receive the previously agreed-upon services and placement until the differences with the current IEP are resolved. Specific implementation of "stay put" may differ from state to state.

When the Team determines after thoroughly reviewing all evaluation information that the student is not eligible for special education services, the school district is required to provide written notice to the parents, which our state refers to as the N1. The written notice shall be easily understandable, record the reason for such finding, list the meeting participants, and notify the parents of their rights to appeal the school district's decision in accordance with state and federal requirements within 10 days of the Team meeting. The federal regulation requires that the written notice contain statements that do all of the following:

- Describe the action proposed or refused by the school district.
- Explain why the school district proposes or refuses such action.
- Describe any other options considered by the school district and the reasons for rejection of those options.
- Describe each evaluation procedure, test, record, and report used by the school district as a basis for the proposed or refused action.
- Describe any other factors relevant to the school district's proposal or refusal to act.
- Explain procedural safeguards.
- List sources for parents to contact to obtain assistance in understanding procedural safeguards.

This aspect of the evaluation process is a crucial element of communication among Team members, including you. Team members need to fully understand the ramifications of determining a student ineligible for special education services as the referring party will likely not be pleased. To assist a student when found not eligible, your district needs to establish regular education interventions that can be communicated to parents to inform them that the needs of their child found ineligible for special education will be addressed in their current classroom. This gets back to the Regular Education Initiative or RtI support.

Your work as an administrator involves communicating with your superintendent and principals so that the district can develop and put in place interventions and strategies for students who require support but are not eligible for special education. This will mean taking a proactive approach, which can lead a parent not to reject their child's IEP; remember that parents have the right to reject the IEP presented to them (or the finding of no eligibility) for their child in whole or in part and request due process in the form of a facilitated Team meeting, mediation, or a hearing related to eligibility, evaluation, placement, or the provision of special education services.

Districts with developed comprehensive RtI models have in place Registered Education Service Plans (RESPs). A RESP allows the district to outline in a brief format the needs of the student, the regular education intervention to be provided, who will deliver the intervention, and the frequency and duration of the intervention. This type of documentation provides the parent with an outcome from the Team meeting and ensures that the student receives support through regular education interventions on a consistent basis. This RESP also provides documentation of the district provisions and can remain in the student's file for future reference during transition from one grade to the next.

The 2004 reauthorization of IDEA brought several changes. From a financial standpoint, the law allocated 50% of new federal special education dollars to general education—a major shift, as most ASEs controlled the rollout of these funds—meaning potential competition for spending these funds within the district. With an additional change related to student eligibility, the reauthorization no longer allowed Teams to use the difference between intellectual ability and achievement as the sole determination when evaluating a disability for eligibility purposes. Many districts had utilized ability and achievement as the criteria for making decisions, and now they needed to establish additional components for the Team to consider. The reauthorization expanded the timeline for assessing a student to 60 days at the federal level, and no longer mandated reevaluations. The change also mandated the assignment of an Educational Surrogate Parent for a student when warranted and reemphasized the lack of reading, math, or language skills as insufficient to determine a disability. Compliance was another area of focus, as was enhancing the process for assessing compliance.

Confidentiality is a mainstay of protecting student and family information. To reiterate our approach, we chose to ask staff to think of the sensitive information they knew about a student or their family and consider how they would want the same information, if it were about their family or their child, to be handled. We always reminded our staff of stories overheard in the teacher's room or out on a soccer field and simply asked them to think before they shared student information regardless of their location.

Visibility Throughout the District

We addressed this issue in the Preface, but it requires additional emphasis. All too often a crucial mistake that we have seen both current and past administrators make is not being visible. The lack of visibility will only lead to problems, so *make yourself leave the office.* Create a schedule whereby specific schools expect you on specific days, either monthly or quarterly, and adhere to it with few exceptions.

Keep in mind that no one in the district knows what you do. They think you just sit at your desk, waiting for them to call with a problem for you to fix. If either of us received a call from a teacher or principal, we made it a point to go to the school either that day or the next day on the way in or as soon as otherwise possible, even if it meant rearranging our schedule. Obviously, in larger districts, this is not possible for the individual in charge, so you will need a system of delegation to the appropriate staff member, as such large districts contain layers of middle management positions whereby you need to ensure that the individuals occupying these positions get out to their assigned schools. In these larger districts, the ASE needs to learn to delegate to those charged with managing the district schools and/or programs. Delegating is the easy part, while making sure that the task has been addressed is the difficulty. When you do find yourself delegating a task, be sure to establish a way to follow up and not lose sight of your goal. Remember, you ultimately have the *R*.

"Who has the *R*?" Simply put, who has the responsibility? Throughout our careers, we often found ourselves in a position where someone expected us to take responsibility for various tasks, and one of our superintendents would ask, "Who has the *R*?" As we have noted, no one knows what you do, and that means many people make assumptions regarding your responsibilities. You may know that when you *assume*, you make an "ass out of *you* and *me*." The goal is to eliminate assumptions by identifying the *R*; the clearer your procedures, and the more open your communication with your staff and fellow administrators, the clearer the *R* becomes.

It may have just been our style, but we wanted to look the person in the eye and get ourselves informed on the matter at hand. We developed a quarterly visitation schedule to walk through each school not only to visit with our staff, but also to connect with the building principal and general education staff as well as the school secretary, the custodians, cafeteria staff, and other school-based staff. This walk-through practice enabled us to be visible, address any building concerns, pay attention to our staff, and gain a greater understanding of the culture of a particular school. It also allowed us to press for solutions that might work in the school rather than finding a solution in isolation or without any involvement at all. Visiting the schools also gave us an opportunity to stop by every classroom, meet students, and introduce ourselves to all the special education staff in the school. Face-to-face always beats phone, text, or email. Also take the time to meet general education staff. If you know the student(s) in a classroom, pay a visit; if a teacher raises concerns about a student, speak to the teacher and if needed arrange to observe the student in their classroom. Obviously, as mentioned earlier, the size of the district predicates your ability to engage in this activity.

Once again, our goal was to listen as well as validate the work of the staff. Getting to know your students is important but not an easy task, particularly when you serve in a large district. We found that stopping by every classroom whenever we visited a school helped us get to know a number of the students. We also got to know many students by name over the years. Obviously, in larger districts this practice may be impractical if not impossible for the ASE. So, it is imperative that middle managers within the department conduct this activity regardless of their role and assignment. When you do find yourself in a position to delegate this responsibility, you must ensure that all members of the department understand the "chain of command." You do not want your middle managers to be viewed in a negative manner simply because they are visiting classrooms.

Departmental/Staff Meetings

Meet regularly with your staff. Keep them informed of what they *need* to know. They have a difficult job, and sharing information not relevant to their work could cause them unneeded stress. Assure them that you are listening to their needs and will do your best to address them. Do not lose sight of any issues they share, and make sure to put them on the next agenda. Value the time you spend with your staff, and always use it to share only pertinent and useful information. You can provide a good deal of the routine updates through a newsletter or email, but when you gather with your staff, be sure that they would not prefer you to communicate the information in another way. Remind yourself that your staff have a difficult job, and each minute is important. This reminder further allowed us to constantly keep in mind that people need to hear or do something

25 to 30 times before it becomes an expectation or routine—even more important when you need to share important updates and expectations.

Related Service Providers and Itinerant Staff

Be sure to meet with related service providers and itinerant staff on a consistent basis as part of your monthly or quarterly meetings with subgroups within your department. These individuals bring unique needs and perspectives to the group but often feel as though they are on the outside looking in. They, too, have difficult jobs and unique needs to address but can feel like you never hear their concerns or consider their recommendations a priority, so keep in mind that their concerns are priorities for them. This group of individuals who provide direct specialized skills to the identified student population includes, but is not limited to, school adjustment counselors, school psychologists, speech and language therapists, occupational therapists, physical therapists, behavioral specialists, inclusion specialists, and Team chairpersons.

School Nurses

Should a part of your responsibilities cover school nurses, keep in mind that they are licensed, which may require them to view a situation differently than the school administration would prefer. School nurses may be regulated by your state's department of public health and hired through the city or town department of public health. Either way, they serve in a position that is vital to the district as a whole and especially vital to special education given the increasing number of medically fragile students coming into schools from early intervention. The school nurse's role has become very cumbersome over the last 20 years and will continue to do so as more medically involved students, students with behavioral health needs, and students with psychiatric needs are integrated into the schools. These very dedicated individuals who now play a more crucial role in the life of the school by maintaining the health of more students on a daily basis must be more vigorously supported. They have become an asset to many Evaluation Teams when confronted with cases of complex needs, and their talents and expertise have proven to be of significant value especially in the era of COVID-19.

Paraprofessionals

Paraprofessionals are an essential part of the service delivery plan for many students with different abilities. In many situations, these individuals provide the bulk of instructional support to a student or group of students during the school day at all levels. Depending on the school district's location, paraprofessionals' degree of experience, skill set, and formal education may vary. These individuals are asked to take on substantial responsibility and often given limited training and support. It is essential that these individuals receive the necessary support and training to fulfill their assigned position.

Teachers usually did not begin each school year with a new paraprofessional, and all too often we received a call in late September or early October informing us that the "para" was just not working out. We just as often found that because the current para did not do what the previous para had done, the problem lay in the teacher's expectation that the new and old paraprofessionals would have a similar skill set. We found it important to assist teachers with this, so we began to introduce the issue as part of the school-year opening meeting. We asked all teachers, even teachers with a returning para, to take time before the start of the year to meet with their para and establish ground rules, alerting the para to the teacher's expectations and the para's role in the various activities of the school day. Without establishing these expectations, when the teacher asks the para to do something after the start of the year, the para may not receive the request in the way the teacher intended. Better to discuss this early on than once daily routines and expectations have been established. This is of utmost importance in programs that require toileting, to set out the teacher's role and the paraprofessional's role before any "finger pointing" begins is essential. You and your school district must find a way to make time available for your teachers and paraprofessionals.

Establishing well-defined roles and responsibilities for the paraprofessional position is crucial for providing clear guidance to paraprofessionals and teachers. It is imperative that paraprofessionals receive professional development training at the time of their hiring and as they work in their position not only to learn their roles and responsibilities but also—and equally important—to understand their assignment.

Office Support Staff

Your secretaries play a significant role with your workload and communications. Both of us feel truly fortunate to work with wonderful secretaries throughout our careers. They monitored our phone calls and incoming mail, and they set the tone for teachers with a clear understanding of the entire process from referral to IEP and beyond. They also set the tone for our office by how they interacted with and treated parents, staff, and others when they entered the office or in a phone call. We wanted our secretaries to completely understand our expectations within the office as well as for the staff. Establishing a clearly defined system so that all parties know your availability and how and when they can reach you eliminates someone saying, "I can never reach [your name]," or "I don't know where [your name] is." We know that today, with cell phones, email, and text, everyone feels that they can contact you at any time. Still, your secretary and office staff need to prepare the appropriate response when a staff member or parent calls your office to complain that you have not gotten back to them. The fact is you could be attending a Team meeting, mediation, a hearing, or an administrative meeting, or out visiting schools, and your office staff should be primed to relay a positive explanation regarding your availability and an approximate time for a response.

Technology Department

Again, depending on the size of the district, the technology department may comprise two or three people or a very large number of staff. You will interface with this department to accommodate the needs of your staff in providing instruction and to assist the students who due to their identified needs may rely on computer assistive technology, speaking devices, specialized software, and other such tools. The staff of this department can be an asset not only to the students but also to the special education instructional staff in providing quality assistance in their specialized instruction. The technology staff, for example, can help identify specialized programs and equipment to assist the population of students with special needs at all levels within the district. With virtual instruction and learning, districts purchasing Chromebooks and other technology related to student learning, and teachers utilizing Google Classroom, staff and students find themselves requiring much more assistance from the technology department. A solid working relationship with your technology department will benefit your staff as they navigate the student data system in the district as well. New staff in particular will require training on the data process as well as the IEP process, and putting together a solid orientation and training for your staff will be very beneficial.

Follow Up

Always get back to others with a response. The easiest way to lose credibility with your staff, parents, and fellow administrators is to not respond in a timely manner. As indicated previously, listening to them, supporting them, and responding to their needs is of primary importance. Always return emails, phone calls, and texts within a reasonable time frame with staff, administrators, parents, and other interested community parties. Your responsibility is to your constituents, who make up the school district and the community. Being unavailable is not an option. In a training that we attended on the skills required of a good administrator, we learned the great significance of determining priorities. One aspect of the training required the potential administrator to go through their inbox of mail and correspondence from the previous day. As observers, our task was to determine how they set the priority related to each communication they reviewed, and when we saw some put off the most controversial correspondence, we learned to always address this first.

We also learned from this experience that you must learn how to manage your time so that you can respond to the various forms of communication in a timely manner. If the volume of communication gets too intense due to the size of the district, then you need to set up a chain of communication with designated staff acting as first responders, second responders, and so on. Once again, the ability to delegate tasks is of great importance, but the challenge comes in following up to ensure appropriate handling of the task. This then makes follow-up one of the top priorities that you must work into your day. Needless to say, for us, getting back to individuals became *the* top priority. In one of our districts, as noted earlier, the superintendent used to ask, "Who has the *R*?" when he wanted to know who took responsibility. So, as ASEs, we spent a good deal of time with our staff and the district's leadership Team clarifying who "had the *R*" for various tasks and requirements. We remembered that throughout our careers, particularly when we assumed a position of delegating. Simply because you have delegated a task does not excuse you from being the responsible person (the *R*). The more all district staff and administrators understand their responsibilities, the easier they will find working as a school system rather than a system of schools.

Responding to Your Staff

Make sure to equip staff with everything they need to get their jobs done—right down to pencils. Teachers, itinerants, and paraprofessionals take on the difficult job of putting all of their energy toward providing the best possible instruction to their students. Acquiring the necessary resources to do their jobs is not a concern they need to consider. Take care to support your office personnel—they work hard with little recognition.

Recognize the needs of each school be they staff or student related. Regular communication with your staff will allow you to remain on top of any concerns they may raise, and always thinking of them as your allies will give you the opportunity to develop a strategy to address the issues they share. As stated earlier, your staff need to live and work in their school, so it is important that you hold their confidentiality and never leave them "out to dry"; always develop a strategy to achieve what you need before bringing the issue to school leader(s).

Distribute a quarterly newsletter to all your staff and to the school administrators with updated information on practices and policies from the state education agency, reminders for staff to comply with regulatory practices and timelines, and so on. Because such information must get from your office to your staff in a timely manner, you may choose to provide a quarterly information update, an effective approach to alerting staff to seasonal activity requirements and indicating who must do what by when, such as Medicaid schedules, budget information, and transitional activities. This essential continuity of practice ensures consistency among the various schools and programs in your district. You never want to hear that at this school they do something one way and at that school they do it in an entirely different way.

Reminders

At the beginning of each school year, we shared a list of reminders with all staff (see Appendix VII), including reviewing student files, maintaining professional relationships, being aware of time constraints, communicating, and documenting. Once again, we reviewed these reminders at various times throughout the school year, knowing that many staff needed to hear or do something 25–30 times before the practice becomes routine. Reviewing these reminders took thought as we once again reminded ourselves that time was everyone's enemy and we needed to utilize it wisely. We knew some staff would appreciate the reminder(s) and others would view it as a waste of their time. Again, set priorities. If all the reminders do not require review, then go through the list and share only those about which you still hear concerns from staff.

Continue to communicate your basic philosophy with your staff—in particular those who chair Team meetings. They are the face of the department for all initial referrals. Take the time to review your beliefs and expectations by reminding staff not to talk about a student in front of them; to develop relationships with general educators, building principals, and above all students and parents; to never make promises they cannot keep; to refrain from discussing finances at a Team meeting; and to keep Team members focused on their area of expertise. Chairpersons play a difficult role as they go about beginning the meeting and conducting introductions, keeping track of time at the meeting, ensuring that everyone feels heard, confirming that parents understand the process, allowing staff to focus on their area of expertise, and closing the meeting in a productive and positive manner. Beyond this, they are responsible for writing the IEP, meeting all timelines, following up with parents and the special education office, and more.

Articles of Information

Provide articles of information to your staff and articles targeted to specific specialists within the department on a regular basis from the numerous available professional journals. All department staff must be kept informed and updated on current research in the field of special education, issues of legal matters, and court decisions regarding practices, as well as state department of education policies and practices. As the ASE, you are responsible for keeping your staff informed and up to date.

Stay on top of current assessment measures, instructional practices, and curriculum initiatives to ensure that identification of students who require special education remains valid, and that instruction continues to meet the needs of your students. State and federal initiatives are also important to ensure that your district remains current with legal requirements and is not at risk in any way of potential compliance concerns. Be sure to take advantage of training or grants made available through your state or the federal government.

Transition Activities

Do not lose sight of transitions. Over the years, we found that transition times brought exceedingly high anxiety for everyone involved—parents, teachers, and, of course, students. In late January or early February, we began meeting with teachers, in each school, to discuss students who would be moving from preschool to kindergarten, elementary to middle school, middle to high school, and high school to adult life. We had two primary goals: first to educate staff on the services available for the student at the next level, and second to alert staff to student needs as they arose. Teachers often believe that no one can service their students as well as they can, so to alleviate this, we wanted staff to know what kinds of services would be available for the student. By sharing the service delivery, we wanted to put teachers at ease to boost their confidence when speaking to parents and, more importantly, informing students of their new placement. During these meetings, we also assured parents that when they asked their children's teachers about availability of services for their children the following year, the teacher could give the parents a well-informed answer. You want to avoid the "I have no idea" or "I don't know what they do" (at the next level) response to a parent's question as this response only heightens, when the goal should always be to lessen, parental anxiety.

IDEA stipulates that beginning at age 14 or sooner, if determined appropriate by an IEP Team, school-age children with disabilities are entitled to transition services and measurable postsecondary goals—a significant requirement that must be met. We know of districts that did not meet the indicated age requirement and were required to provide compensatory services.

Many parents have found themselves in the position of reeducating staff each year about their child, and we made it a point to share that with staff at the beginning of each school year and at transition time. When staff began servicing a new student, we expected them to read that student's file. We never wanted to hear "I didn't know that" when a parent asked the staff person a question, or "the teacher didn't know this about my child," particularly when the information appeared in the student's file. This response would lead to the parents questioning everything that staff person did with their child from that point on. Sometimes it may also benefit students to visit their new setting and "shadow" the class for a day to fully prepare them for the next step in their education. For some students, you may also want to arrange a meeting between the child's parent(s) and new teacher and/or administrator prior to the start of the school year to talk about challenges, strengths, and strategies previously seen to work well for their child.

Transitions are a time of high anxiety for parents, students, and teachers, whether from one grade level or school to another, graduation from high school, or turning 21–22 and moving from school life to adult life. While we will discuss the transition to adult life (Chapter 688 in our state) in Chapter 12, the importance of developing relationships with your state's human service agencies is critical to assisting your staff and parents to see a clear picture of what lies ahead. Parents often found it hard to hear that once their child reached 21–22, they would lose the protections of special education law with its entitlement to a free and appropriate public education (FAPE). In Massachusetts, human services for adults are "contingent upon appropriation" from the state legislature.

Maintaining a written document for the district that spells out the steps to the annual transition process such as who by position is responsible for what, timelines, and transition meetings between levels is essential. The sending school sets the goals and benchmarks, while the receiving school develops the schedule and frequency of services. This reduces the issue of students getting lost in the system and allows the sending staff to fully understand the services available for the student the following year. Further, it allows the receiving staff to gather the needed information on the student to assist them in the intricacies of the new learning environment.

Another significant transition for staff, parents, and students occurs when a student returns from hospitalization. When a student leaves the hospital, school personnel often believe they are "cured" or "fixed" before returning to school, but unfortunately this is not the case. When one of us was developing an alternative program, we hired a psychiatric nurse to work in the program, and she explained that when a child enters a psychiatric hospital setting, the hospital staff peel back the layers to get to the core of the problem that the child is exhibiting. The hospital staff then re-lay those layers, and the work begins to keep those layers in place. Too often school personnel are not informed of the work the student puts in while hospitalized and in fact are guarded as they recall the student and what led to the student's hospitalization, and they expect the student to repeat the same behaviors upon return to school. Many school districts offer a transitional program for these students as they return to school. Whether you have a program in place or not, educating and informing staff on the student's status and progress made, as well as efforts they can make to ease this transition, is essential.

CHAPTER SUMMARY

Your position comes with a great deal of responsibilities. Ensuring not only that your staff have what they need to do their job but also that students get what they need to succeed is an ongoing responsibility that requires your continued attention, whether in the form of materials, curriculum, or trainings for various staff to deliver what students require. Your job is to protect the district, ensuring that all compliance expectations are met, and this means sharing with staff all legal expectations. To that end, your job also involves the interpretation of laws and regulations for administrators to make them aware of any potential consequences if the district fails to comply with the state and federal government's regulatory expectations. Remember that a person needs to hear or do something 25–30 times before it becomes a part of their routine. You may need to list a task on the agenda for several staff meetings, allowing your staff the opportunity to internalize your expectations. Do not get discouraged or impatient if staff do not perform the way you expect the first time.

Try to remind yourself that no one has all the answers, and be willing to admit you do not know. Again, make it a point to respond with the clarification or answer being sought. Years ago, when the laws and regulations required a great deal of interpretation, we were fortunate that technology, as we know it today, was not part of the culture. We communicated in person, via phone, and through "snail" mail. Today everyone wants, and expects, an immediate response to their email or text, and if for some reason the recipient does not respond immediately, they feel slighted. Routine questions come up every day—as we indicated in the Introduction, 100 balls in the air and 500 questions—so answer those as best you can, but if an issue is other than routine, allow yourself 24 hours to digest and prepare your response. Parents are not the enemy. Always, always be respectful of parents; after all, you are here to serve their child. You may not like or agree with their approach, but you should respect it. Just as the process indicates that the IEP Team makes decisions to benefit the student's special education needs, the process also allows for parents to disagree with the Team's recommendations.

In addition to your difficult cases, your budget, and the current trends coming to your district from early intervention, your collaborative, and private school students, you should get to know your transportation providers. We have ridden in vans and met with drivers who have shared our concerns. We have also learned that if your gut tells you to take action, you should do it and ask for forgiveness later. The pace of your day can be daunting, and most days fly by. If you stopped to ask state agencies or others for direction, you would constantly trail behind the proverbial eight-ball. Be confident that you know your business, and if you do not, then learn it. Someone will always correct you so you know to do it differently the next time. Do not try to "reinvent the wheel." Instead, call another ASE to seek assistance; your colleagues face many of the same or similar situations as you do, so utilize their expertise and invite them to draw from yours. Becoming a member of a collaborative is a particularly good place to begin the process.

ALWAYS REMEMBER

- Prior
- Preparation
- Prevents
- Poor
- Performance

We lived by this simple rule throughout our careers. For every meeting we attended, every phone call, email, or text we made or returned, we prepared in advance. We would review student files, talk to individuals with knowledge of specific situations, prepare for anticipated responses, and, as we have indicated, document, document, document everything. We cannot repeat this reminder enough: Remind your staff to summarize, *in writing*, every conversation regarding student progress, status, and concerns for further reference. Keeping a written record that summarizes the content of discussions and resulting agreements will be of substantial benefit at some point during the school year. As the ASE, you should always follow up a parent meeting with a

(Continued)

letter or email to the parent summarizing the outcome of the meeting including the issues resolved, those remaining to address, and who is responsible for each. This type of document can prevent confusion and misrepresentation later.

All along, we remembered that we were the "duty experts," and if we were asked a question for which we did not have an answer, we informed the questioner that we needed time to investigate and get back to them. Be sure to provide a specific period for your response. This will assure the individual of your commitment to addressing the issue and give you the time to gather the information for a thoughtful response.

The professionals identified in this chapter have evolved over the years to become an integral part of the special education Team. They require support not only from the department and building administration, but also from the district with respect to specialized professional development specific to their needs. A calendar of specific training and information must be in place to ensure current training and awareness by staff of the evolving needs of the student population. Many students come to school with special needs—medical, social, and mental health—that must be addressed by the school nurse. Because current professional development is essential for all staff to function, we will pay more comprehensive attention to professional development in Chapter 10.

Always remember, after all, that this is only a job. One of us kept a quote attributed to Dick Johnson, dated 1991, in our office: "How many times have you spent a long night eyes wide open as you stared into space, dreading what's coming tomorrow, filled with fear over what you must face? RELAX. You'll find it's almost always true that the final realization is really nowhere near as bad as that awful anticipation." Do the best you can, do what's best for the children you serve, and remind yourself that there's life beyond work. When an ASE new to the position asked one of our colleagues, "When does the job get easier?" our colleague responded that the job is the job, and it never gets easier; you simply find ways to work smarter. Early on, when we often worked 12-hour days and went into the office on weekends, one of our wives asked over dinner, "Is that all you think and talk about?" referring to a one-sided conversation about work. We made a promise to ourselves after that observation that we would talk to ourselves about work all the way to and from work but never again at home, except for the good stuff that happened for our students. We also realized that we needed to prioritize and endeavor to work "smarter"; we limited weekend work, for example, to one day a week for only a few hours. The work will never go away, whether you work an 8-hour day or a 24-hour day. Your goal is to strike a balance between life and work. On the days when you say to yourself, "How can I keep doing this?"—and you will have those days— remind yourself that it's "only a job," someone has to do it, and today that's you. According to another saying one of us kept in the office, "One day I sat musing, sad and lonely and without a friend, and a voice came to me from out of the gloom, saying 'Cheer up; things could be worse!' So I did cheer up, and sure enough, things got worse!" Find a rose to smell, or visit a preschool classroom (*any* classroom, for that matter). One of our brothers always encouraged us to "go to our happy place," and we advise you, too, to find your own happy place and relax. Work, after all, is work, and life, after all, is life!

8 Inclusion

A great deal of discussion has already occurred regarding the inclusion of students with disabilities in the general education environment. Volumes of research literature, from the early 1970s to the present day, exist on the subject of inclusion—a child's right to participate in all general education classes. While some believe that all students, regardless of the degree of severity of their disability, should be served in general education classrooms full-time, others believe that inclusion means servicing a student in the Least Restrictive Environment (LRE) to the maximum extent appropriate for that individual student. A strong antidiscrimination climate has led the charge for full inclusion, and proponents reject special schools and separate classrooms. The law, the Individuals With Disabilities Education Act (IDEA), has a strong preference for students to be involved in the general education environment (LRE), and a clear statement is required justifying the student's removal from their general education class(es). The law also requires a full continuum of services and programs to meet the needs of identified students. For some students LRE will be general education with supports and services to ensure effective progress. For others it may require removal from general education for periods of time during the school day, and for others it may require full removal from general education and placement into a self-contained class, a separate day setting, or a residential facility.

Few would disagree that students with disabilities benefit substantially from inclusion in general education classes and programs when appropriate and feasible. Because both populations of students benefit socially from inclusion, it is important to continually monitor the educational progress of students in special as well as general education classrooms. Inclusion, with appropriate supports and services, is the goal; however, when the Team determines that a student is not making effective progress given the available supports and services, inclusion may not be the appropriate approach to meet the needs of this student. As we discussed earlier, the initial regulations emphasized "mainstreaming," or educating students with special needs in a regular education classroom when the Team determined that they could benefit from the instruction provided in the class. Over time, mainstreaming has been replaced with inclusion—the reverse of mainstreaming. This approach places students in the general education classroom where they are taught general education curriculum until they no longer benefit from the instruction. In the early days of the law, serving general education students in a special education classroom or other setting was not allowed. Over time, this "paradigm" has shifted toward what many refer to as reverse inclusion, placing general education students in special education classes for both instruction and social interaction.

Thinking of inclusion as a philosophy, rather than a placement or setting, will assist you in navigating the discussion of inclusion as both a philosophy and an approach to serving students with disabilities from low to high need. Inclusion involves the establishment of systematic approaches that enable districts, individual schools, and classrooms to create an environment that includes students with disabilities in the general education settings within their school and community. Inclusive practices that focus on instructional and behavioral strategies for improving the academic, social, emotional, and behavioral health needs of all students will enhance the opportunities of students with disabilities, regardless of the degree of disability, to experience a full education in the LRE. For any form of inclusion to succeed, the district must provide adequate supports and services for teachers and students along with professional development. Once again, depending on the population of students, the district may need to consider reducing class size and allotting time for teachers to plan together (common planning time) to achieve successful inclusion. Finally, the district must remember that inclusion may not work for all students, some of whom may still require a separate environment to meet the goals incorporated by the Team into the student's Individualized Education Plan (IEP).

When many districts first began heading in the direction of inclusion, we observed several districts do away with all their self-contained (substantially separate) programs. At the time, many of us saw this as premature since the districts did not develop their inclusive philosophy and plans before deciding to educate all their special education students, full-time, in general education classrooms. Within two months of the opening of the school year, administrators of special education (ASEs) were making calls looking to place students in surrounding districts or collaborative programs. As we have indicated, deciding to build and place students into programs is just as significant as deciding to move students out of programs and how to facilitate that transition. Of particular importance is the need for receiving teachers and administrators to know as much as possible about the student(s) as well as the services and supports made available to ensure effective progress.

Ask the following questions about inclusion in your district:

- Is inclusion required for all students?
- Is inclusion a legal requirement?
- What are my district's beliefs relating to inclusion?
- Does everyone in my district know what inclusion is?
- How does my district implement inclusion?
- Does everyone in my district understand their role in an inclusive classroom?

As the ASE, you cannot fear inclusion. Instead, you must embrace the opportunity to create an inclusive environment in each school and classroom across your district. Revisiting your beliefs about educating students with special needs will support the work required to assist all school-based staff with getting to an appropriate place for the district.

Developing guiding principles regarding inclusion is the first step to ensuring clarity among all school-based personnel and building administrators. This task will take time, but time well spent to create a dialogue of thought and understanding about what you, as the district's lead ASE, want to create. Similar to Strategic Planning or Facilitated Discussion strategies, the outcome is a unified mission and vision statement that provides the building blocks to a philosophy for inclusion.

In his article "The Death of Special Education," Laurence Lieberman (2001) speaks to the federal movement toward inclusion and away from the "individual" student. The push to provide every student with the general education curriculum in the general education classroom has seen special educators move away from remediation of individual disabilities to supporting the general curriculum. A former colleague of ours was well known for saying, "I don't want my special education students in a regular education classroom simply to breathe regular education air"; he wanted his students to receive the specialized instruction required for them to make effective progress. A student's identified disability may impact the amount of inclusive time that the student can participate in. Interestingly, different countries vary in their beliefs regarding inclusion; in the United States, for example, 60% of students identified as having a learning disability spend the majority of their time in general education classrooms while in Denmark 99% of students with learning disabilities, including dyslexia, receive their services in general education.

Putting in place standards and rubrics that represent established practices will assist you greatly in the follow-through of the work of educating students with special needs in an inclusive environment. As we started out in the mid-'70s, we began by building programs that pulled students from their general education setting to receive services or establishing programs considered substantially separate (self-contained). Many of these programs were built for the purpose of increasing district capacity to maintain students with special needs within the district. Tuition for out-of-district placement at collaboratives and private day and residential schools began to increase at significant percentages annually, and the cost of placement once considered reasonable became annually increasingly more expensive.

In the mid-1980s, the thinking began to change as more research emerged that students with disabilities can be educated in general education classes if appropriate supports and services are put forth. Legal cases also supported this thinking, and the trend began to take hold in the early '90s for students with significant special needs to benefit from experiencing instruction in a general education classroom with their peers for greater portions of the school day.

So where should you provide services to students deemed eligible for a special education? Students can receive these services in the general education classroom, in a pullout special education setting, in a self-contained classroom within the school district full-time, or outside of the district in a collaborative or private special needs day or residential school. Full inclusion is not a part of existing law; rather, LRE, with appropriate services and supports as indicated, is the mandate of the existing law. We have seen just as many examples of inclusion working very well as examples that appear not to work at all. The key to positive inclusive experiences for students is the belief not only that all students can learn but also that they are entitled to receive services in the LRE. This belief must start at the top with the superintendent and expand to all building leaders. Leadership must have a comprehensive understanding of inclusion, the district's plan for implementation, and everyone's role in the process. The first question is, do all leaders understand their role? And the second question is, do all staff understand their role? To achieve successful inclusion for students and for staff, you need to go beyond the expectation and make it a part of the school culture.

Servicing and including students in the LRE has become a primary goal of many school districts over the past decade. In our state of Massachusetts, statistics for the 2020–2021 school year indicate that 79.7% of students were either fully included (66.2%) or partially included (13.5%). The reported percentages become the goal for most districts; some districts report higher and some lower percentages, but most districts measure their efforts to include students against the state percentage. Of the remaining 20.3% of students, 13.6% attended self-contained programs, 2.9% public day placements, 2.7% private day placements, 0.6% residential placements, and 0.5% home or hospital programs. These percentages also become the measure for districts when they look to see how many of their students are serviced in substantially separate classes or private special education schools. As we write this, many states continue to rely on pullout programming as they move toward an inclusive culture.

We focused on other statistics in our work over the years. Each year, for example, we tracked down the percentage of students serviced in special education in our state (for the Fiscal Year [FY] 2019 school year it was 18.1%, for FY 2020 it was 18.4%, and for FY 2021 it was 18.7%), and then compared the state average to our district average and the averages reported by our surrounding districts. We also kept account of the economically disadvantaged students receiving services in special education and enrollment of minority students. This annual review allowed us to focus on areas not in line with state expectations as well as inform program and service decisions that might be required.

General educators are considered the experts in their curriculum area. The integrity of the general education curriculum cannot be replicated by special education personnel, and that should be a driving force when considering the inclusion of students with special needs in general education classes. Response to Intervention (RtI) has a significant place in ensuring that general education provides *all* students with the services they need to remain in their LRE and assembling data to support a special education referral when warranted. Interventions prior to a referral are significant, and principals' involvement is especially important. RtI is the current focus for activities prior to referral, and again it is important to continue to focus on questions like the following:

- What does RtI look like in the district?
- Does everyone understand the process?
- Is it consistent throughout the district, or does it differ from school to school?
- Is everyone clear on their role in the process?

When all staff clearly understand these questions, a district is moving to ensure that prereferral/RtI efforts become part of the culture for each school and the district as a whole.

RtI takes a tiered approach, as shown in Figure 8.1. The most used teaching strategies and interventions (good teaching practices), found at the base of the table, is called Tier 1 (the primary level of failure prevention), reach about 80% of students. Tier 2, the secondary level of prevention, appears in the middle section, where the interventions become more intensive because the students are at a greater risk of failure. About 15% of students will comprise the Tier 2 section at any given time, and only about 5% of students make up Tier 3, or the tertiary level of prevention, found in the top row of the table. Here, students receive the most intense and consistent interventions. Although Section 504 (part of the Rehabilitation Act of 1973) prohibits discrimination based on disability, 504 plans and special education are both associated with this tier. Note, however, that not all students in Tier 3 are covered under a 504 plan or receiving special education services with an IEP.

Substantially separate programming will always be needed, as will collaborative, private day, and residential programming, but inclusion should be the foundation of our practice to ensure access by students with disabilities to the LRE along with the necessary support(s) to make the experience successful.

Figure 8.1 Response to Intervention (RtI)		
BEHAVIOR		**ACADEMICS**
Intensive Interventions • Development of an individual behavior plan • Scheduled monitoring • Consideration of a referral for a special education evaluation by the problem-solving team	**Tier 3** **5%**	**Intensive Interventions** • Customized instruction with annual goals and frequent monitoring • Consideration of a referral for a special education evaluation by the problem-solving team
Targeted Interventions • Small-group support focused on appropriate behavior and social skills interventions • Progress monitoring focused on behavioral/social skill development	**Tier 2** **15%**	**Targeted Interventions** • Small-group instruction in the classroom • Monitoring to determine the effectiveness of instructional changes • Consideration of additional concentrated intervention time
High-Quality Differentiated Classroom Instruction • Standard high-quality instruction differentiated as needed for the student • Established procedure for identifying students who are exhibiting social-emotional behavioral health needs that could affect their performance in the classroom	**Tier 1** **80%**	**High-Quality Differentiated Classroom Instruction** • Standard high-quality instruction differentiated as needed for the student • Established procedure for identifying students at risk based on their academic performance

Co-teaching

To properly operate co-teaching and other in-classroom instructional support models, you need to establish clear, concise, and agreed-upon statements that stress the purpose and intent of these two separate models of instruction. As indicated earlier, research indicates classes should comprise two-thirds typical students and one-third students receiving a special education, students with 504 plans, or English learners (ELs). The state of Illinois has a 70%–30% regulation covering the makeup of inclusive classrooms. When special and general education teachers come together, they must be allotted common planning time to work on curriculum and develop an understanding of the students and the curriculum expectations. Are staff familiar with and utilizing, for example, principles of Universal Design for Learning (UDL), Positive Behavioral Interventions and Supports (PBIS), and social-emotional learning (SEL)? In our experience, the most productive co-teaching is achieved when the two collaborating teachers remain together for several years. Co-teaching plays out like a marriage, with various ups and downs, and when teachers must team up with a new partner on an annual basis, these ups and downs may keep repeating, which impacts students and the learning environment. When Teams remain together, year after year, they can work out the instructional practices and their individual roles in providing seamless lessons and instruction to students. In examining numerous co-teaching models in many school districts, we identified successful co-teaching Teams that had been collaborating for many years. Obviously, Teams that work together for short periods of time can also achieve success, but the point is that collaborating teachers need to remain together to become a collaborative Team.

As previously noted, the general educator is the curriculum expert whose knowledge and understanding must be acknowledged and appreciated. The special education teacher brings the full knowledge of the student(s) with special needs and how their disabilities impact their learning. When both teachers accept their role and share in the instruction, then co-teaching becomes seamless and productive, which allows the teachers to keep an eye on the two populations of students, general and special, to ensure that they progress as anticipated.

Pushing In

The roles and functions of a special education teacher and the special education support staff assigned to a general education classroom need to be clear and understood by all. How will itinerant personnel provide their services in the general education classroom? What should be expected from teaching assistants in the classroom? What is the role of school leaders and parents? As noted earlier, the laws began with primarily pullout services, and mainstreaming initially meant that students would return to the general education classroom when ready to assume the challenge of the general education curriculum. Today, many students remain in their general education classroom with the required supports and services, which allows them to benefit from the curriculum along with various special education personnel entering the classroom to provide their services. We have seen many examples of these services benefiting not only the special education student but also general education students. This occurs when both the general education teacher and the special educator understand the curriculum and the individual students' needs and expectations. We have also seen special educators assigned to a table in the back of the room to work with "their" students. This leads to isolation and clear identification of the students with special needs. Further, it does not allow for general education students to benefit from the special educator's expertise.

One main reason for providing pullout services was the cost-effectiveness; one special educator, for example, could work with several students from several classrooms and even from different grade levels. Push-in services, on the other hand, are not cost-effective as they limit the special educator to one classroom and only the identified students therein. Inclusion, be it co-teaching or push-in services, clearly costs more than pullout as it requires more staff. The inclusion approach requires you to establish stringent procedures and expectations for all involved teachers, paraprofessionals, itinerants, and administrators. Each school principal must understand the role they play in evaluating "your" staff, and if they need clarification on inclusion and how to implement inclusive instruction in the classroom, then they will make ill-informed decisions and risk compromising the intention of these important services for students.

Dr. Seth B. Harkins (2012) provides an excellent literature review on inclusion in *Inquiry in Education*. This comprehensive article, "Mainstreaming, the Regular Education Initiative, and Inclusion as Lived Experience, 1974–2004: A Practitioner's View," provides the reader with not only a historical perspective, but a look into the struggles facing administrators and educators regarding the debate over inclusion, as well as the struggles that school districts faced and are still facing in addressing the social, political, and research pressures to move toward a more inclusive education setting for all students with disabilities. The article provides an understanding of the forces behind the inclusion movement while giving credence to the need for professional development for all building administrators and school-based personnel to enable them to facilitate inclusion more effectively at the building level. Dr. Harkins also relates his own experience in a new school district and the initial efforts to develop it from the beginning into an inclusive school district—an example of what you can accomplish when everyone, from the superintendent on down, agrees on the philosophy of inclusion as the primary approach to educating students with disabilities.

CHAPTER SUMMARY

Numerous competing interests will arise when developing an inclusive environment that will support your philosophy of inclusion. From determining the number of special education students who should be enrolled in a classroom, to calculating student-to-teacher ratios at the various levels throughout the district, specialized services will be provided in general education classrooms, to Title I students, and to the population of students receiving free and reduced-cost lunch within each school and throughout the district. These and many other factors influence the degree of inclusion that may or may not occur within a district, but regardless of the challenges, you are responsible for embracing inclusion to benefit the population of students with special needs. Should your district support inclusion to a high degree, it may be difficult to maintain with reducing resources and increasing cohorts of students with more significant needs. Many believe that inclusion is an inexpensive approach to servicing students with special needs. In fact, inclusion is expensive to implement as you must provide the specialized instruction and services and the staff to deliver the support in the general education classroom. Providing students with these services in a separate environment may be cost-effective, if one special education staff member can service several students from multiple classrooms, but such separation continues to create a stigma of isolation for students with special needs.

9 Programs and Services

Options and Choices

Keeping your eye on trends related to special education diagnosis and service is essential in preparing your district to serve students in the Least Restrictive Environment (LRE). In the early years of the law, a great many programs were developed at the local district level for students with developmental, behavioral, and intellectual disabilities. In recent years, programming for students on the autism spectrum and students with social/emotional/behavioral health needs has been a focus. The early 1990s brought a new medical diagnosis of pervasive developmental delay—not otherwise specified (PDD-NOS), and many of us believed it was just that—another medical diagnosis to address students with developmental delays. When we began to observe students with this diagnosis, it became clear that the characteristics we were observing did not match what we had traditionally observed in students diagnosed with a developmental disability. The same dynamic occurred with students identified with Asperger syndrome; these students displayed characteristics we had not observed previously.

In their article "The Misdiagnosis of Special Education Costs," published in *School Administrator*, Sheldon H. Berman and David K. Urion, MD, wrote in 2003 that district practices have no bearing on special education expenditures, but medical and social factors accelerate spending. The article speaks to, among other things, the impact of premature birth on special education: "Primary among these causes are changes in medical practice. Medical technology has advanced to such a degree that children who would not have otherwise survived due to prematurity or disability now live well beyond their school years. In addition, those whose disabilities would previously have placed them in institutional settings now can enter public schools or private special education schools" (Berman & Urion, 2003). These authors' work also references the significant increase in students diagnosed with autism in the state of California. A study conducted by the University of California (M.I.N.D. Institute, 2002) did not find any evidence that the rise in autism cases could be attributed to artificial factors, such as loosening of the diagnostic criteria for autism. Districts not keeping an eye on these trends found themselves scrambling to locate programming for students with these diagnoses along with emotional disabilities.

An article from the early 1990s indicated that in California the identification of students with autism had increased by more than 200%, a trend that appeared to be working its way across the nation. In one of our districts, the only student identified as autistic aged out of services in 1980, and for the next 14 years, not a single student in the district received an autism diagnosis. By the mid-1990s, many administrators of special education (ASEs) were preparing for programs to serve students with autism should the need arise. As you begin the process of developing quality programs, it is important for qualified experts or consultants to guide you and participate in the program in the early stages of servicing students. When we look back at programs we worked to develop for students with hearing impairments, students with autism and emotional or behavioral health needs, and preschool students, we remember the individuals we sought out to assist and assure us that we were utilizing the most current research and evidence-based practices to achieve our goal of quality programming. Over the years, experts such as Dr. Robert Ferullo, the chair of the speech and language department at Northeastern University, and the late Dr. Joseph Powers and Dr. Russell Ricci from McLean Hospital, along with the May Center, Landmark Outreach Program, and Boston College Campus School, assisted us in development of various programs and provided strong oversight and services to these programs.

We have also looked on as our colleagues developed private–public partnership programs by bringing private school personnel into their district to serve a specific group of students. We contracted with private schools for students with special needs, including Boston College Campus

School, the Cotting School, the Carroll School, the Gifford School, Walker Partnerships, and The Guild School, and counseling centers, such as Colony Care Behavioral Health and Beaverbrook Guidance Center, to provide direct service to various programs and ongoing consultation by individual experts to program staff on an ongoing basis. Collaboration with these agencies benefitted the districts by ensuring that we remained current in our practices as well as in dealing with emerging trends and issues affecting these specialized populations. This collaboration also allowed districts to remain focused on serving students in the LRE.

Each year, it is just as important to review students who might receive services outside of your district to determine if you can start a program to return them to the district. Our rule of thumb is that if you identify three students in need of services, then you should look to develop a program. When you factor in the cost of sending three students to schools outside of the district, including both program and transportation costs, these funds should go a long way toward program development. Personnel, material, and potential transportation costs are easy to calculate; however, the human factor requires the most attention. In addition to determining where to locate the program, you must work with school leadership to ensure that they support the program and, more importantly, that they will support the program with their own school staff.

We know many ASEs who identified a need, built a budget, and moved forward without ever addressing the human factor by seeking out the support of the school leader and their staff. Overlooked factors might include fire drills; for students who are not mobile, for example, will staff be identified to assist them? Will the students be included in special activities like art, music, and physical education, and if not, will they require a separate art, music, or physical education class that will warrant additional staff? Besides these two examples of needs to address at the building level when developing a new program, the school administration or personnel might bring other ideas to the discussion when a new program is under consideration for their school. We are aware of several instances where an ASE went through the effort of developing a program without involving either school or special education staff, resulting in a program population of students and staff who felt alienated within the school and not embraced when moving forward the needs of the students to the administration or general education staff. Some of these programs survived simply through the will of the special education staff, and others proved unsuccessful, forcing the students to face another transition within a short period of time. We have discussed to a great extent the importance of principals and school leaders becoming a part of the mission and belief that all students can learn, and that students with with different abilities have a great deal to add to their schools. Each principal also has their own beliefs and leadership style, and your challenge is to convince them of the importance of developing a culture to serve all students and that serving students with special needs in the LRE is achievable in their school.

One of us was working with a new ASE when he asked us to look at a PowerPoint presentation. He was very excited to be presenting to the school committee on a new language-based program at the elementary level. As he began showing the PowerPoint, when asked who else participated in the development of the program, he responded, "Well, we need it." So, again he was asked about staff involvement, the school where the class would be located, and the principal of the school supporting the program. To these, he answered that no other staff had been involved, the superintendent told him they would find a classroom, and the school and principal had not as yet been identified. In our experience, developing a program in isolation will inevitably lead to problems. All constituents need to be involved and invited to share their thoughts and concerns. School staff need to be informed and perhaps educated on the intent of the program and the attending students. Art, music, health, and physical education need to be engaged to ensure that the new students can receive services. The principal needs to support the program and be prepared for existing staff to embrace the new program's students and staff. The parents of the designated students need to be informed and brought along in the process as well. Their engagement is crucial to the enrollment of theier child and their support for the programming.

A program may be "needed," and you can shape the discussion for a positive outcome by involving everyone. The last thing you want is to establish a program in isolation and watch as the students and staff become isolated once it begins. A few days after our discussion with the new ASE, he called to let one of us know that he was holding back from moving forward with his presentation to the school committee and was in the process of establishing a committee to "look into" the possible need for a language-based program.

One of the key factors in development of a program is to establish both entrance and exit guidelines. All constituents must clearly understand the population to be serviced, how decisions are made to enroll a student, and how to determine that a student may transition from the program, and a program brochure is always beneficial in outlining these guidelines. We have seen instances of the lack of entrance criteria or guidelines leading to the placement of students who do not meet the service requirements and therefore jeopardize the quality of the program. Once you have identified the need for and addressed the many aspects of developing a program—budget, staffing, supplies, and materials—the involvement of all key constituents becomes essential. One of our superintendents would remind us that "water always reaches its own level," meaning that if you start a program, it will fill up; "if you build it, they will come."

We continued to remind ourselves that keeping the program population consistent with the initially established program mission and goals was a difficult job. Staff would assume that the program could service their student. Your job, working with staff, is to set clear criteria for determining not only how a student enters the program but also, and just as importantly, how a student exits a program. How will these transitions take place?

The laws continue to require a full continuum of services to be available for identified students. This means when new program development is indicated, regardless of the size of the district, you must have options to address the various needs of students. Even if all programming is offered in-district, the programming map for your district must provide you with choices for serving the variant needs of your district's students. One size does not fit all. What makes programming successful is the comprehensive approach to development. Plan so that the initial offering includes everything you need. Try to stay away from building a program or service over several school years. You may not have that opportunity if resources are restricted in any given year; however, while the process can take time, depending on district resources, proper planning will ensure you have put in place quality defensible programming and services.

Your district may be large enough to offer an array of programming at each level for many or even all of the disability categories, or your district may have too small a cohort of students in many disability categories to develop program options for all. Should you serve in a smaller district, you may rely on surrounding districts, collaboratives, or private day schools with greater program options (including tuition and transportation cost considerations). Either way, you need to constantly build your continuum of programming and service offerings based on census and disability categories of identified students so that your district can serve the needs of its special education population from preschool to 21 or 22 years of age.

Students Returning From Hospitalization

Each year, a number of students are hospitalized for various medical and mental health reasons. Particularly for students in the hospital for mental health treatment, it is important that everyone serving the student realize that the student returning to them may very well not be the student who left. A psychiatric nurse explained to one of us that when a student enters the hospital, it is like peeling back the layers of an onion, and the work of the hospital staff is to reach the core and then reapply the layers. Many school districts have developed programs to transition students out of hospitalization, which allows staff to bring the student back to their classroom is as positive a manner as possible. Many staff will keep in mind the behaviors of the student before leaving, and programs like this allow them to get acquainted with the student and their current performance.

Compensatory Services

COVID-19 has brought about a new focus on compensatory services. As indicated, a student's Individualized Education Plan (IEP) is a contract outlining required services, and when a district finds itself unable to provide a service, the missed service may have to be made available for the student in the future. This often happens when a service provider leaves at some point in the school year and the district cannot find a replacement in a timely manner, and then compensatory services come into play. Your state's department of education likely developed procedures throughout the COVID-19 era to guide you. A pandemic, however, is not the only time to concern yourself with possible compensatory services. We are aware of districts required to provide compensatory services for significant amounts of time due to procedural violations, some of which related to the district's failure to provide services and others to missed required timelines. In one situation, the IEP Team for a student turning 14 did not discuss transitional needs, and the parents rejected the IEP into the following year. At the conclusion of due process, the district was required to provide a summer program to include work- and training-related services for the student. The district had argued, to no avail, that the student did not require such services; however, the fact that the district acknowledged its failure to discuss transitional needs at the IEP meeting was a compliance violation impossible to explain away. So, be aware of procedural and compliance requirements that, if not adhered to, could lead to compensatory services.

Restraint

The more school districts develop programs to serve students within their local schools, the need for potentially restraining students increases. Individual state laws as well as the federal law address restraining students; the U.S. Department of Education (2012), for example, published a document to provide guidance to states and local districts. Your state likely also requires training in restraint techniques to utilize should the student indicate the need for restraint. As we recommend throughout this book, seek out any guidance made available by your state's education department to assist you with making proper decisions when training and informing your staff. You may also choose to discuss this with your legal counsel. A number of techniques and programs cover de-escalation and physical restraint, and your state may favor particular programs or develop their own guidelines to assist you and your staff. Obviously, physical restraint is the last resort when working with a student; always choose a de-escalation intervention first. Time-out is another technique that districts utilize, and again your state likely requires protocols for conducting this intervention, such as having eyes on the student at all times. The safety of students—*all* students—is the priority in any school, and a full and clear understanding of protocol on the part of all staff and administrators will go a long way to ensure student and staff safety as well as that the district has taken all precautions.

Quality of Staff

The quality of the staff for all programs and services is without question the key to quality instruction and student success; the staff you hire can make or break a program. In vetting the staff before hiring them, be sure they present with the right temperament for the particular program or service that you are considering them for and that they have the knowledge and skill set to do the job well. Keep the following factors in mind:

- Be sure to speak to their most recent employer. To review a résumé or view a working journal is one thing, but it is another thing entirely to speak to someone who can relay to you their impressions of the individual and answer your specific questions.
- Assess their experience; have they worked with the specific population of students you have in mind?
- Consider their experience with assessment as well. What specific programs have they utilized in their work?

- Most importantly, consider the extent to which they value their work and their students.

- If you have any doubts regarding the individual's ability, skill sets, knowledge, temperament, do not hire the individual; move on to another candidate.

Taking these factors into account will allow you to make an informed decision and determine if the individual will be a good fit for your department. You do not want someone to walk into your office after the first day of classes and say they cannot do the job, hand you their resignation, and insist they will not return.

Program Evaluation

Program evaluations are required by law and an expectation of the monitoring conducted by the state educational agency. An evaluation can greatly benefit you by pointing out areas of focus to improve not only your service delivery but also the communication required to enhance understanding of all aspects of your programs. Be sure to determine whether all staff understand their roles in servicing students. Have you made clear to everyone the expectations of newer positions such as Board Certified Behavior Analyst (BCBA®) or behavioral specialist?

Have you developed program brochures that contain clear entrance and exit guidelines? Do staff understand the decision making for placing a student into a given program or outside of the district? In our experience, without this the program will lose focus and ability to successfully service the primary intended population.

Consider, too, whether transition processes are clear, be they how a student enters or exits a program or moves from one level to another such as preschool to kindergarten or middle school to high school. A time of high anxiety for all involved—the student, the parents, and the staff—transitions can make or break student success.

Is program oversight and supervision in place to ensure that programs serve the appropriate student population? An evaluation will also assist with the maintenance of staff schedules, allowing you to see potentially available times in the day to add services or employ a one-to-one paraprofessional should the need arise. A note on one-to-one paraprofessionals: Do all involved understand the process of deciding to provide a one-to-one paraprofessional? Will it be clear when the student no longer requires the assistance of the one-to-one paraprofessional? What will that transition look like?

Many benefits can be gained from a program evaluation, including information about the functioning of a program or related service; any obstacles facing the program, services, and staff; additional needs of staff; the types of professional development needed; and steps you as the ASE should plan to ensure that all programs and related services meet their stated mission. We have spoken at length about communication, understanding, and consistency, and to that end, we strongly advise you have an up-to-date and easy-to-understand special education handbook. The handbook will allow your staff, along with principals and general education personnel, to work from the same message when addressing special education matters—be it paperwork, timelines, staff roles, parent involvement, student assessment, the Team process, timelines, or any other component of this complex process.

Educational Services in Home or Hospital

Still another program consideration involves students in the hospital or confined to their home. When your district receives a physician's written order verifying that a student enrolled in a public school or placed by the public school in a private setting must remain at home or in a hospital on a daily or overnight basis, or any combination of both, for medical reasons and for a period of not less than 14 school days, the principal shall arrange for the provision of educational services in the student's home or the hospital setting. Such services shall be provided with sufficient frequency to allow the student to continue their educational program. The principal shall coordinate such services with the ASE for eligible students. A student does not require an IEP to receive such educational services as they are not considered special education unless the student has been determined eligible for such services and they are included in the student's IEP.

Home- and Incarceration-Based Services

A neutral site, if staff will ever be alone with students, is yet another responsibility to be aware of along with providing services to students confined to the home or hospitalized for medical reasons. When this occurs, a doctor must provide written documentation indicating the need and the possible duration. You will be required to provide tutorial services to the student until they return to school, and your state may follow a specific procedure for home- and hospital-bound students. Your state should also have procedures to cover educational services to incarcerated students.

Your Responsibility to Homeless Students

The McKinney-Vento law governs services and transportation to students considered homeless. Your district is required to employ a homeless coordinator, and your primary concern will be to ensure all efforts are made to continue provision of services to displaced students with IEPs.

CHAPTER SUMMARY

There is an exception to every situation, but extablishing sequential practices, procedures, policies, and programs will greatly reduce the possibility of error on the part of building administrators, school-based staff, and your department personnel. A procedural manual will require periodic review and updates as practices and policies at the local, state, and federal level change. One proven approach is to establish a study group to undertake this task, consisting of a cross section of staff from key positions within the department; district size will determine the appropriate number of staff and their positions. The group needs to comprise a sampling of department personnel including direct service providers, program supervisors, Evaluation Team chairpersons, school psychologists, social workers, general education personnel, school principals, and, of course, yourself.

Program and service development is the lifeblood of your department. Building quality defensible programs and services can be exciting and extremely rewarding. But to be effective, you need to do your homework and work from the five *P*s. The cost benefit of instituting a new program or service clearly must be part of the goal, but most important is identifying students with similar disabilities who need to receive services within the district; as indicated, having three students with similar needs is enough to call for developing a program. You need to bring together the staff who can help identify trends in the student population from early intervention programs to your own in-district programs and services intended for your current and emerging student populations. In building program and service capacity you must design the program based on evidence-based practice and, with the cooperation of central office and building administrators, use all assets of the district

(Continued)

to bring to fruition your intended program(s) and service(s). Developing a program needs to follow a true Team process with all voices heard and all concerns considered and addressed. Do not attempt to develop a program in a school dominated by a culture of "us versus them."

We learned early on when developing a program for students with hearing impairments that several factors required consideration. First and foremost, what philosophy of instruction does the student require (signing, oral, or whole language)? Second, for any student who requires the assistance of a device for hearing, a good audiologist must be available to service the devices and provide support to staff and parents. We were very fortunate to have a quality professional audiologist to guide us through this process and also be available to staff and parents.

As noted, we have seen both productive and less productive ways to develop programs. In one district, the out-of-district coordinator assessed that the population of students receiving services outside the district could return if a program was developed internally. The out-of-district coordinator brought this information to the ASE, who then went about building a budget, ordering supplies, hiring staff, and consulting with a principal to access space or a classroom for the program. The coordinator then set up Team meetings for the three students with the intention of writing IEPs to return them to the district. This meant hiring teachers and putting supplies in place before holding the Team meetings, and a classroom was identified but the principal failed to inform the staff currently utilizing the room that they had to move. The real concern occurred when two of the three parents did not accept the proposed IEP to return their child to the district, which meant that the program staff would be servicing only one student—all because the ASE did not do their due diligence with the parents as part of the process of program development. Parents of anticipated students must be included in the discussion of program development especially when you may recommend a change in placement. Without parental buy-in, all your efforts can go for naught. Again, we emphasize the Team approach and the five Ps anytime you are looking to develop a program successfully.

Professional Development 10

Between us, we have conducted well over 250 individual building, program-specific, and district-wide special education program evaluations. We have had the great pleasure of interacting with so many great professional educators who have provided us with open and forthright knowledge of their experiences with building-based and district-wide professional development. Here we are, 40-plus years into both the state and federal special education laws, and we have yet to see a school district meet all expectations of these laws. Many districs have put forth good effort, but the effort is a continual one for school districts to strive to fulfill the expectations of the state and federal laws. Too often we hear about the "us versus them" of general and special education, and the ownership issue continues to concern many administrators of special education (ASEs) at the building level—that is, the lack of efforts prior to referral of students, referring to students by their "program" instead of by their name, and the view of programs as separate rather than a part of the school fiber. We hear from special educators that they are required to attend trainings that have little or no relevance to their role or their work. Time for special education training is not often made available, and providing such training through department meetings with any degree of consistency is not productive. Once again, the question is, how will you ensure time is utilized to benefit your staff?

Providing professional development is a constant challenge. With all the curriculum and other initiatives that general education takes responsibility for, how does special education fit into the overall district-wide picture, and can districts find the time to address the needs of special education staff? We are all aware that time is the biggest enemy of all educators and needs to be utilized with great focus and efficiency. How do you go about providing the training required for your special education teachers, your itinerant staff, and your paraprofessionals? If you use the time to bring them all together, are they all getting what they need? Do psychologists, occupational therapists, speech and language pathologists, school nurses, paraprofessionals, and others need to learn what you have developed for your special education program teachers, or do each of them have different training needs? The same can be said for your teachers: Do they all need to learn what the general education teachers are learning about various initiatives, or are their training needs different?

So where do you begin? We suggest you start with the person in the district charged with setting up professional development. Is it the superintendent, the assistant superintendent, another director, or each building principal? Get the "lay of the land" and go to the source to plead your case for accessing professional development time for your staff as well as time with general education staff. As ASEs, we often utilized the analogy of the bicycle wheel, with the student at the hub and each person working with the student a spoke. If one of the spokes is not working properly, then the wheel *may* not run smoothly; if more than one spoke is not working properly, then the wheel is *certainly* not running smoothly. If the student represents the hub and each staff member serving the student a spoke, then staff should know the role they play to keep the entire wheel running smoothly, in balance. How do general education staff learn how to assume ownership of students on Individualized Education Plans (IEPs), and what is the role of the special education staff and paraprofessionals working with students in the general education classroom? How do they learn their roles in servicing the various needs of the student population, particularly students on the autism spectrum and students with behavioral, social, or mental health needs? If each staff member (or spoke) plays a role in the overall achievement of students serviced with an IEP, you must ask yourself, and others in leadership roles, whether providing them with the training they require is a priority.

What do staff look for? We hear from staff, from both general and special education, that instruction in some topics would greatly assist their ability to work with students. Examples of staff requests for professional development include the following:

- Understanding of special education requirements, practices, and procedures for all school-based staff.
- Eligibility process.
- Specialized instruction, including how it differs from other forms of instruction.
- How to write IEPs with measurable goals and benchmarks.
- The co-teaching model of instruction.
- Current trends in special education.
- "How to" teach and instruct the various disability categories of students with special needs in general education classes.
- Specific disabilities and their characteristics.
- How each type of disability impacts learning.
- Servicing the various needs of the student population.
- More types of instructional interventions and strategies for specific disability categories.
- Training for itinerant service providers to provide greater push-in services.
- Training on addressing students' mental health issues.
- Dealing with anxiety and the subsequent behavioral dysregulation.
- Managing challenging classroom behaviors.
- Trauma and the impact on learning.
- Understanding the effects of trauma and how to create a trauma-sensitive classroom and school.
- Culturally responsive teaching.
- Equity for students with IEPs.
- Training in Zones of Regulation, Social Thinking, and Second Step for new staff (with a review for principals and current staff).
- Crisis prevention intervention and de-escalation strategies.
- How to make push-in therapy time doable and effective.
- Executive functioning and how it impacts learning.

- Conducting functional behavioral assessments (FBAs).
- Writing positive behavior intervention plans (BIPs).
- How to deal with difficult Team meetings.
- Training on facilitated Team meetings.
- How to effectively communicate and collaborate with parents.
- Classroom data collection applications for teachers and paraprofessionals.
- Assistants using technology for IEPs.
- Assistants using technology for data collection.
- Effective and simple data collection using apps.
- Section 504.
- Determining which staff require continuing education units (CEUs) to maintain their license.

Numerous training videos are available to share with staff, and we want to mention a few with an exceptionally long history that continue to bring home a valuable message when shared. Richard Lavoie's (1989) video "How Difficult Can This Be? The F.A.T. City Workshop," provides a comprehensive look into the learning experience of children with learning disabilities. He shares many messages that impart to all involved—general and special education personnel, administrators and parents—a clearer understanding of life with a learning disability. His definition of fairness, "Fair is when everyone gets what he or she needs," dispels the notion that taking a different approach to teaching and learning for disabled students is unfair. A principal once told us that when he shared this video with his faculty, it made an impact unlike anything he had seen in his 20-plus years in his position.

Joel Barker's (1989) video "The Business of Paradigms" keeps a focus on the future. As special education leaders, you must continue to look ahead and remain current with servicing and programming for your students. Barker also reminds us, as noted in the Introduction, that "when a paradigm shifts, everyone goes back to zero."

"Educating Peter" (Wurzberg et al., 1992), another highly informative video, follows the experience of a young student with Down syndrome in an inclusive classroom. The film presents this experience through the eyes of Peter as well as his classmates and his teacher. We can all learn from the insights shared by the various parties as we go about placing students, providing the required supports to meet students' needs, and once again listening to and learning from those engaged in the learning process.

We believe school staff and their colleagues will benefit from an understanding of these topic areas, among many others. School-based staff well recognize the challenges facing educators today with the focus on curriculum frameworks, standards, and high-stakes assessments for determining students' acquisition of skills and knowledge. However, we also understand that in most school districts 15%–20%—and even as much as 26% in urban settings and communities with high cohorts of low socioeconomic standing—of the student population are receiving special education services. Not focusing on and providing time to train the staff serving students with an identified disability who are eligible for special education puts these students at risk of not adequately meeting these high standards. We have kept our focus in this chapter on students receiving services through an IEP. We have not addressed students on 504 plans, which we covered in Chapter 5, or students with Limited English Proficiency (LEP). We assume that these two groups of students receive their services through regular education systems.

CHAPTER SUMMARY

Professional development for all district staff is an ongoing and continuous activity for all school districts and must be well planned out each school year. The format of professional development should focus on a series of sessions over a designated period that enable staff to drill down into content, learn necessary strategies that will benefit them in their classroom or teaching situation, and assist staff with changing instruction strategies and providing students with a high-quality instruction. Professional development is necessary for staff to experience training that can support each of them, regardless of their role, for improving their instruction to students with special needs. Professional development will also provide them with insight, awareness, and appreciation for the students in their care. With an in-service program rich in content and instructional as well as behavioral strategies, school-based staff will

(Continued)

grow and improve in their presentation of curriculum and support to students, which will assist in improving the outcomes for all students. Determine before the beginning of the school year when you will have time to provide your staff with professional development. In our experience, special education staff are required to attend general education trainings, but the ASE has no time allotted throughout the year. Once again, your relationship with the person in charge of the professional development calendar will give you a voice and allow you to determine how to support general education personnel with their understanding of special education. When your state agency conducts compliance monitoring, you never want to be in a position where they come back with "The staff needed training, but it was never offered!"

Discipline and Students With Special Needs

11

The protections in the Individuals With Disabilities Education Act (IDEA) regarding discipline are designed to prevent abuse to the right of students with disabilities to receive an appropriate education. As discussed in *Mills v. Board of Education of the District of Columbia* (1972), the court recognized the exclusion of many children from education merely because of an identified behavior disorder. Keep in mind that the protections granted in the law do not prevent school officials from maintaining a safe environment conducive to learning for all children. We have found that schools with good leadership, well-trained teachers, and high standards for all students experience fewer discipline problems than other schools.

Disciplining special education students can cause concern, and educating your staff and more importantly your administrators is important to ensure that students' rights are maintained and that neither the district nor the student is at risk. Disciplinary concerns most often occur at the secondary level although on occasion they arise at the elementary or middle school level. Although we do not want to belabor this topic, we will provide a good deal of detail in this section. The provisions of the statutes and regulations concerning the amount of time a student with a disability can be removed from regular placement for disciplinary reasons only come into play if the removal constitutes a change in placement. If students without disablities would be subjected to removal for an offense, then school authorities may unilaterally suspend a student with a disability from special education placement. As the Supreme Court ruled in *Honig v. Doe* (1988), suspension must not exceed 10 school days at a time for any violation of school rules.

Of course, in the case of less serious infractions, schools can address the misconduct through appropriate instructional and/or related services, including conflict management, behavior management, and measures such as study carrels, time-outs, and restrictions in privileges, so long as they are consistent with the child's Individualized Education Plan (IEP). If a child's IEP or behavioral intervention plan (BIP) addresses a particular behavior, it's generally inappropriate to utilize some other response, such as suspension, to that behavior. In instances where the parents object to the proposed action by the school (or object to a refusal by the school to take an action), they have the right to request a due process hearing.

School officials can work with the student's parents when they believe that a placement is inappropriate. If a student exhibits behavior problems that interfere with learning (their own or the learning of others), the IEP Team must consider whether strategies, including Positive Behavioral Interventions and Supports (PBIS), are needed to address the behavior. If the IEP Team determines the need for such services, they must be added to the IEP and be provided accordingly.

The IEP process should be utilized to come up with an appropriate placement for the student that will meet their needs and provide a safe learning environment for all. In addition, responsible and appropriate changes in placement of a student with disabilities are allowed when the student's parents do not object.

Changes in IDEA emphasize the need of state and local educational agencies to ensure that superintendents, principals, teachers, and other school personnel are equipped with the knowledge and skills to appropriately address behavior problems when they occur. From our experience as ASEs and conducting many special education program evaluations, we have found that when teachers and other school personnel have the knowledge and expertise to provide appropriate behavioral interventions, future behavior problems can be greatly diminished if not totally avoided. Professional development activities, as discussed in the previous chapter, can help to ensure that regular and special education teachers and other school personnel receive the needed knowledge and skills.

Even when school personnel receive appropriate training and proactively address students' behavior issues, in some instances they must remove the student from current placement. The discipline provisions of the law need not be brought into play when school personnel and the child's parents agree regarding a change in placement.

Should the parents disagree, school officials can still remove any child with a disability from regular school placement for up to 10 school days at a time whenever discipline—consistent with that of students without disabilities—is appropriate. No specific limit exists on the number of days in a school year that a student with a disability can be removed from current placement. However, when the suspensions start to form a repeated pattern, school officials must determine whether the student's IEP is appropriately meeting the student's needs, but they cannot use this authority to repeatedly remove a student, for example if the student received several suspensions for the same offense, such as fighting, talking back to teachers, and so on.

When a district removes a student from their current placement for more than 10 cumulative school days in a school year, the district must provide services to the extent required by law for students suspended or expelled from school.

When a student requires change in placement, school authorities can unilaterally remove the student with a disability from regular placement for up to 45 days in an interim alternative educational setting (IAES), or "45-day placement," under IDEA, and this is considered a change in placement if the student brought a weapon to school or to a school function, knowingly possessed or used illegal drugs, sold or solicited the sale of controlled substances while at school or a school function, or is substantially likely to injure self or others in regular placement. The district can remove the student under these circumstances even if the child's parents do not agree to a change in placement. You may need to check if your state provides for any additional circumstances that exceed the federal law.

If at the end of an interim alternative educational placement of up to 45 days, school officials believe that returning the student to regular placement may be dangerous because the student is substantially likely to injure self or others, they can request a due process hearing to advise that the student remain in an interim alternative educational setting for an additional 45 days. The federal law also allows school officials to request subsequent extensions of these interim alternative educational settings for up to 45 days at a time if school officials continue to believe that the child is substantially likely to injure self or others if returned to regular placement. In some states, however, the state law does not allow for the 45-day extension, so you will need to determine how your state directs you to react should this occur.

School officials may seek a court order to remove a student with a disability from school or to change a student's current educational placement if they believe that maintaining the current educational placement is substantially likely to result in injury to the student or others. And finally, school officials can report crimes committed by students with disabilities to appropriate law enforcement authorities to the same extent as they do for crimes committed by students without disablilities.

Beginning on the 11th cumulative day in a school year that a student with a disability is removed from their current placement, the school district must provide those services determined necessary by school personnel to enable the student to appropriately progress in the general education curriculum and appropriately advance toward achieving the goals set out in their IEP. School personnel will determine where to provide those services. This means that for the remainder of the removal, which includes the 11th day, and for any subsequent removals, services must be provided to the extent determined necessary. The school administrator or other appropriate school personnel should be involved in the determination of services in consultation with the student's special education teacher.

You must convene an IEP Team meeting to develop a behavioral assessment plan unless you have already conducted a functional behavioral assessment (FBA) and implemented a BIP for the child. This must occur no later than 10 business days after removing the student for more than 10 school days (in the same school year). When the student removed for the 11th cumulative school day already has a BIP, you must convene the IEP Team to review and modify the plan and its implementation as necessary to address the behavior.

A manifestation determination is not required unless the removal that includes the 11th cumulative school day of removal in a single school year is a change of placement.

CHAPTER SUMMARY

Disciplining all students always requires a good deal of thought, and when a student happens to receive services on an IEP, it requires even more. Once a student is determined eligible for special education, they are covered by all aspects of the law(s). You are then required to ensure that all district administrators (superintendent, assistant superintendent(s), principals, and assistant principals) understand fully their role when disciplining a student in special education. This includes timelines to meet (remember the 10-day rule from *Honig v. Doe*), manifestation determination and how it is made, when to consider an interim alternative placement, and what constitutes a change in placement, among others. Be sure not to leave your district in a nondefensible position when these issues need consideration. You always want school administrators to contact you if they have any questions. The relationships you develop with each of them should ensure this communication takes place when indicated. In the realm of discipline, you never want administrators to make a wrong decision.

12

Age of Majority and Transition to Adult Services

Federal special education regulations require that *at least one year prior* to a student's 18th birthday the student and their parent(s) must be informed of the rights that will transfer from parent to student when the student turns 18, the *age of majority*. Differently titled agencies in all states provide age of majority and adult services. The significant factor is that local school systems are required to begin the transition process two years before a student graduates or turns 21–22 years of age, depending on your state's age requirements. Planning for this transition has become more comprehensive and time sensitive since students are leaving entitlement services for adult services not guaranteed or entitled. Administrators of special education (ASEs) must establish clear processes to ensure that when a student does transition, the district has fulfilled all of the required obligations to enable the young adult to transition smoothly.

When students age out of special education in our state of Massachusetts, the next step in their life journey is frequently not solidified. Most often, students will rely on a state agency to make services available; in our state, for example, a piece of legislation known as Chapter 688 is intended for *students in need of continued services as adults*. Students with severe disabilities, in other states, will access adult service through their individual state's process. Students who receive services in accordance with an Individualized Education Plan (IEP) and receive Supplemental Security Income (SSI) or Social Security Disability Insurance (SSDI) and/or are on the registry at the Massachusetts Commission for the Blind (MCB) are automatically eligible for Chapter 688. Other eligible students may include those with severe disabilities who need continued services and are unable to work 20 or more hours per week in competitive, nonsheltered, nonsupported employment at the time they are ready to leave school. Students who receive services from the Department of Youth Services (DYS) or the Department of Social Services (DSS) and are on an IEP or a 504 plan may be eligible.

Students must be referred two years before they graduate from high school or turn 21 or 22 years of age. Should a district file late, the student's eligibility for services after leaving the school district may be jeapordized. Only school systems can refer students believed eligible for adult services through Chapter 688. As the ASE, it is important for you to cultivate a relationship with the various state agency representatives responsible for receiving the referral of a student for transition to the appropriate state agency. These individuals want to do right by these young adults, and we have found in working with them over the years a positive professional relationship benefits all involved.

The two-year planning period allows enough time to determine eligibility for adult services and for state agencies to include the anticipated cost of services for the student in the budget request submitted to the legislature each year. If a student meets the Chapter 688 eligibility requirements, an Individualized Transition Plan (ITP) must be written for the student. Special education services provided while a student is in school are entitlements mandated by federal and state law. Chapter 688 is not a continuation of *or* an entitlement to special education services. The delivery of services identified on the ITP is linked to program availability that depends on funds allocated in the annual state budget, contingent upon appropriation.

Both of us made it a point to get involved with human service agencies as active participants on various boards and attending as many of the agency meetings as possible. We wanted to understand the services available for our students and, more importantly, how to access the services. Being on a first-name basis with agency workers and leaders allowed us to discuss our students long before any transition as well as to educate the agency on how our students would benefit from their services. As indicated, Chapter 688 provides a two-year coordinated planning process for students whose entitlements to special education services will end when they graduate from high school or turn 21 or 22 years of age. The appropriate human resource agency depends on your state; in our state, it would be one of the following:

- Department of Developmental Services (DDS).
- Department of Mental Health (DMH).
- Massachusetts Rehabilitation Commission (MRC).
- Massachusetts Commission for the Blind (MCB).
- Massachusetts Commission for the Deaf and Hard of Hearing (MCDHH).

Agencies such as these work with school districts and gather the required information to develop the transitional plan for the student upon their transition from the public schools.

The federal law indicates that students are eligible for special education services through their 21st birthday or receipt of a high school diploma. Massachusetts law provides services through the 22nd birthday or receipt of a diploma. Other states' laws may cover students once they are no longer eligible for services, like Chapter 688, through their school district. Prior to a student transitioning from the school district, the ITP developed in conjunction with school personnel, parents, students, and the appropriate agencies outlines the necessary adult services. The language of Chapter 688 indicates the link between delivery of services identified on the ITP and program availability dependent on funds allocated in the annual state budget. Specifically, any services offered or provided are *contingent upon appropriation*. Unlike special education law, which *entitles* students to a Free and Appropriate Public Education (FAPE), such language does not exist for students who have aged out of or graduated from special education.

Transitional services formally became part of the law in 1990 with the establishment of the Individuals With Disabilities Education Act (IDEA). The law required that beginning at age 14, or sooner if determined appropriate by an IEP Team, school-age children with disabilities shall be entitled to transition services and measurable postsecondary goals. Transition services, as stated in the law, are a coordinated set of activities that promote movement from school to postschool activities—for example:

- Postsecondary education.
- Vocational training.

- Employment.
- Adult services.
- Independent living.
- Community participation.

You must remind all involved that the transition component of the IEP is just that—a part of the student's regular IEP. It is not a parallel document, a separate document, or a "transition IEP."

CHAPTER SUMMARY

Transition to adult services is a crucial step that requires school districts to put a system in place to ensure that all compliances are met prior to the student's graduation or turning age 21–22. Different states have different requirements for adult services, and each school district must be fully aware of the eligibility requirements, the referral process, time-lines, and services available. This information should also be provided to parents. Remember that as parents they have functioned under an entitlement system since their child was determined eligible for special education. Now, parents may function under a system based on appro-priation of funds, which does not guarantee that their child will receive services upon graduation or turning 21–22 years of age. You have built programs and services for students with significant needs, but now they will move to an adult system that may or may not be able to serve them to the same extent as your district. Transition can be just as difficult for the parents as for the young adult. You must build into this transition process support for parents through workshop presentation or trainings that will provide them with the necessary information, but more impor-tantly the adult support, to successfully maneuver the transition land-scape. Always remember that this is a difficult time for your students and especially their parents. Respect their anxiety as they move from the protection of a free and appropriate education to the truly unknown.

13 Documentation

Documentation is an essential aspect of special education that you need to embrace with vigor. Regardless of the activity, event, or situation with a student's case, parents, staff, administrators, human service providers, school committee members, or community interest groups, always document the outcome for future reference and clarity. When following up with any of the aforementioned groups or situations, you will need to provide documentation that reflects the outcome of discussion; this information later may be required to demonstrate your position, intervention, and explanation of the facts. Documentation cannot be overemphasized in the world of special education, from both a practical and legal perspective toward your responsibility and role.

The extent of documentation that you construct on any given matter or case will enable you to defend, if needed, your position. Failing to keep a documented record of a situation and its outcome leaves too much to memory, which over time may be unreliable. Documentation in written form provides you or your successor with the needed information to ensure that all parties are protected and informed of the outcome of a case. As the administrator of special education (ASE), you need to take notes at all meetings that concern parents, students, staff, administrators, and other interested parties so that you can in turn develop a running record of a case or situation that will provide the reviewer with an accurate account of previous discussion, outcomes, and/or agreements.

We recall hundreds of examples of thorough documentation either "rescuing" one of us from disaster or putting us in a precarious situation. Proper documentation on a case or issue over time can prove extremely beneficial.

Case in point: A complaint was filed with the Office of Civil Rights (OCR) against a school district for violating the rights of a child with special needs to a free and appropriate education. The case had an 11-year history of involvement with special education ever since the child's family moved to the district. Numerous services were put in place, and all were documented through updated and amended Individualized Education Plans (IEPs). Detailed summaries of all meetings conducted either as special meetings or as IEP meetings appeared in the case file. When the OCR contacted the district, they requested a copy of all documentation, assessments, IEPs, progress reports, and communication between the district and the student's family.

This complicated case involved a student with significant learning and emotional needs as well as periodic episodes of trauma. The documentation provided was constructed from the earliest to most current dates and compiled in three-ring binders. In the end, the investigation found no violation of the student's right to an education. This finding, as stated by the OCR, was based on interviews and a thorough review of the documentation provided by the district.

CHAPTER SUMMARY

The enormous benefits of taking the extra time to document all that relates to a case or situation, regardless of how trivial it may appear at first, cannot be emphasized enough. We always found it important to follow up meetings with a written memo or email stating what our notes indicated and closing with a request to let us know if we missed anything or presented anything incorrectly. Once again, documentation—particularly if you proceeded with something that you later learned was incorrect—will allow you to refer back to the summary particularly if the individual receiving the memo or email never got back to you with corrections.

PART III

Working With and Managing Related Stakeholders

14 Parents

Every parent we interacted with throughout our careers only wanted what they thought was best for their child. We indicated in the Preface we chose to treat all of our colleagues with respect until their actions indicated they no longer deserved it. That very same philosophy/belief stood for parents as well. We may not have agreed with what they were seeking or even how they were going about it, but we always respected their advocating for their child. As parents, we also could recall how we and our spouses felt at a meeting for one of our own children, and now as grandparents with school-age grandchildren, we view the role of parents from a new perspective. We always felt butterflies in our stomachs as the ones receiving information, good or bad, on our child. In sharing the same philosophy with our staff, we were aware of the difficulty from the staff's standpoint to respect the efforts of parents whose requests they perceived as unreasonable and who did not agree with what staff thought was right for the student. We always wanted parents to know that we, too, had the best interests of their child's education as our goal even if they did not agree with our recommendations.

How you and members of your department interact with parents is essential in developing and maintaining trust. You want parents to trust that what you are offering is clearly in the best interest of their child, your student. You never want to hear a parent say that they did not feel like part of the Team or "I have contacted Mr./Ms. Jones several times but have not heard back from them." Trust can break down very quickly and very easily. Prompt responses by you and your staff, or the lack of a prompt response, can very quickly raise the parent's already high level of anxiety and begin to instill a lack of trust. Remind your staff members who chair team meetings that parents are just as important as any other member of the Team. They need to allow parents every opportunity to be heard and gather all the information they need from the Team members. As they say, there is no *I* in team, and chairpersons must make sure that parents do not perceive them as the sole decision maker.

As stated in the Preface, we wanted to be made aware if a staff member received pushback from a parent or an advocate. We first reassured the staff member that we supported their position, and second contacted the parent or advocate to ask that in the future they speak directly to us or a designated staff member, not the teacher, about their concerns. We well understand that not all communication is positive, and with texts and emails being sent at all hours of the day and night, responding becomes a very difficult task. One of our attorneys advised that the primary contact receive all correspondence and, if multiple texts or emails are involved, respond at the end of the week—for example, "In response to all of your inquiries this past week . . ."—and then go on to address as directly and succinctly as possible the inquiries. These, too, are difficult correspondence and require a good deal of thought as your goal is to protect the teacher or staff member while maintaining some form of a relationship with the parent and/or advocate.

Parental Involvement/Consent

Parental involvement is a significant requirement of the law and in fact one of its cornerstones. Parent permission is required for virtually every aspect of addressing the educational needs of identified students. With the extent of knowledge available on the internet, parents can very easily access their rights and information about their child's learning needs. Parental consent must be acquired before you begin any aspect of the special education process, including initial evaluation and reevaluation, or, should the student be found eligible, before you provide any services or make an initial placement of a student into a special education service and/or program.

Individual assessment may be waived with the approval of the parents if an equivalent assessment has been recently completed and if the person conducting the school assessment determines that the assessment results remain accurate. All special education personnel assigned to assess a student must make all efforts to avoid duplicative or unnecessary testing. You as administrator of special education (ASE) may agree to waive some or all assessments for a student's three-year required reevaluation so long as such waiver is in accordance with your state or federal law. Keep in mind that a parent may revoke consent for assessment or placement at any time.

Should the Evaluation Team determine that the child is eligible for special education services and that placement in a special education program is indicated, the parents have the right to observe any program(s) proposed for their child.

If the Team determines that not enough information has been provided to make a decision regarding a student's eligibility for services, then an extended evaluation can be considered. When a parent consents to an extended evaluation, the Team shall document its findings; determine the questions to ask during the extended evaluation and the information required to identify the student's needs; address any unresolved issues required to develop an individualized education plan (IEP), if appropriate; and determine the necessary time for evaluation. The Team may decide to meet at intervals during the extended evaluation but in all cases shall reconvene promptly to develop or complete an IEP after the evaluation. The extended evaluation shall not be considered a placement, and may extend longer than one week but shall not exceed eight school weeks.

Parent Advisory Council

The laws require school districts to establish a Parent Advisory Council (PAC) and indicate the role of the district in coordinating these efforts. A functioning and focused PAC can be of great value both to parents and to you as the ASE. Your involvement in addressing the training needs of parents and soliciting their input into budget and other initiatives will allow you to remain current with parents' expectations for your department as well as give you the opportunity to receive input into the direction your PAC is looking to take. Not being actively involved with your PAC can lead to difficulties as parents may assume they play an expanded role in the direction of your department or that you choose not to be involved. This presents the risk of your PAC becoming more of a forum to share individual concerns and take on more of a vigilante role than a supportive role.

Some of our colleagues viewed their PAC as forced upon them. We found that our colleagues who embraced their PAC and worked with parents on common goals achieved much greater success. As mentioned earlier, parents are not the enemy; in fact, many parents are strong allies of the efforts put forth by your staff and your department. In our experience, when things were going well, PACs often found no reason to meet, and on the other hand, when they were not going well, the parents tended to point fingers and look to reshape the direction of the special education department. Our experiences saw us assisting the PAC to coordinate bake sales and other fundraising activities, as well as bringing in speakers from within the district or from supporting agencies outside the district. It was not unusual for one of us to spend a day working the drive-thru at McDonald's or selling various goods at the library. Our goal was for the parents to view us as partners, not enemies.

In one case, a family was not pleased with the services offered by the district to their child. Mediation was attempted to no avail, and the case proceeded to a due process hearing. The student had a wonderful teacher, and the district ended up prevailing at the hearing. We recall two things from that case: First, the teacher, in tears, could not understand how this process took her away from all her other students for several days. Second, many years later, at a donut shop of all places, the mother of the student approached, and we expected her to share the negative impact of the process on her child. Instead, she thanked the district, and described the great experience her child had and all the wonderful special education teachers who taught him, particularly in high school; she also shared that he had been accepted to college and would be starting in the fall. You can never predict how cases will turn out, but if you focus on the needs of the students and what is best for them, you will never go wrong.

Another case involved a young student who was on the honor roll and a cheerleader in her sophomore year. In her junior year, the student was referred for a special education evaluation, and during the assessment the teacher informed us that they believed the student was under the influence of drugs. As the evaluation proceeded, the student was found eligible, and services were provided. The student continued to regress and, at some time during the winter months, jumped out of her bedroom window into the snow and ran. When the student was found, she did not return to home or to school, but was hospitalized. After several weeks in the hospital setting, the student returned home only to run once again. The student was again found and hospitalized for several more weeks and then discharged to a private special education school. The student was the youngest in a large family, and all her siblings had graduated college. In this particularly sad case, the parents were initially reluctant to request any services for their child; after all, she made the honor roll only months before. Once they realized their child required assistance, their concerns continued, but they worked with the school district to find the most appropriate services for their child.

In yet another case, a 5-year-old child was placed at McLean Hospital with a diagnosis of schizophrenia. While driving to McLean, the school psychologist informed us that a 5-year-old could not be diagnosed with schizophrenia as, among other factors, the ego was not developed at that age. After sitting through the meeting—hearing how this child not only witnessed his mother committing suicide but also a year later witnessed his grandfather committing suicide—on the drive home the psychologist said, "OK, maybe after learning what this child experienced, it looks like my theory was wrong."

Noncustodial Parents

A section of the student record regulations in our state, Massachusetts, covers noncustodial parents. In general, a parent is always considered a parent; however, if the custodial parent informs the school that they have sole custody and provides documentation to the school principal, then the parent who does not have custody, *the noncustodial parent*, must make a written request to the principal to review the student's records. The school principal must immediately notify the custodial parent of the request and, via first-class and certified mail, explain that student record information will be shared with the noncustodial parent after 21 days unless the custodial parent provides the school with written documentation of a court order barring the requesting noncustodial parent from contact with the child or of a protective order preventing abuse to the child.

The school principal must redact all electronic and postal addresses and telephone numbers of the custodial parent before providing the redacted student record to the noncustodial parent. We have included this section as an FYI (for your information) to review and potentially help you avoid any conflict between parents, be they custodial or noncustodial, and the school district.

Acronyms

Keep in mind that special education sometimes feels like a foreign language to parents and others; LD, NLD, ED, PDD, ASD, MR, ADHD, IEP, LRE, FAPE, FBA, BIP, and IDEA make up just a few of the everyday acronyms in use, and each state may well have its own frequently used terms that have become part of the daily vernacular. Your staff likely know most, but probably not all, of the acronyms used, and certainly parents, general educators, other administrators, school committees, and town officials know very few, if any. We shared a list called Alphabet Soup (Appendix V) at parent advisory meetings and with school leaders each year to give them some insight on special education jargon and provide them with the knowledge they might require upon hearing these terms.

CHAPTER SUMMARY

Special education legislation brought forth the importance of the parents' role in the special education process. Parental involvement begins with consent to conduct the evaluation and continues through signing the IEP and approving, or rejecting, the services and placement for their child. Essential to your work as an ASE is to unify parents to support your efforts in providing services and building quality programming for the students of the district. The quality of instruction can be improved upon not only through your efforts, but also through the efforts of the district when parents trust those efforts. Our role as educators and ASEs is to make sure parents know that they are a part of the process and provide them with the information and support to understand the process. Be sure to make parents feel like a part of the Team, and remember to have Team members refrain from using

(Continued)

acronyms or, if they do, explain what they represent. Stay away from jargon. Parents can be, and have demonstrated that they are, strong allies of special education and progressive supporters of the development of quality programming. The vast majority of the parents in your district will be pleased with the services provided to their child. Many of our colleagues, over the years, tended to focus on the very small percentage of parents who disagreed with/rejected the district's offer to their child. Those who attack your efforts on behalf of their child may have a hidden agenda unrelated to your efforts for the student. Or, as a student, they may have had a difficult school experience. Obviously, these situations are difficult as relationships with parents are essential to working with and achieving success with their child. Always listen to, be respectful of, show courtesy to, and thank them, particularly when you find it difficult to reason with them. Accept them as part of the process, and do not allow them to bog you down in their issue.

Central Office 15
Administrators

Central office administrators, depending on the size of the district, generally consist of a superintendent, an assistant superintendent(s), and a business manager, as well as individuals responsible for curriculum and instruction, assessment and student outcomes, and special education (student services, pupil personnel services, etc.). Smaller districts may employ only one assistant superintendent who may take responsibility for a host of general education issues. (We continue to acknowledge that large urban districts with a multitude of administrative positions may place the administrator of special education [ASE] near the top of their organizational chart, further removing the ASE from the students and staff.)

Superintendent

The superintendent is a key player in special education. How this administrator supports your philosophy, your mission, and your vision for special education within the district will go a long way toward determining your success. For you to truly succeed, you and your superintendent must have a positive, agreed-upon relationship with regard to all matters involving special education.

Clarity of the ASE Position

Several aspects of the job of ASE require clarification from your superintendent, beginning with whether you are part of the Leadership Team. We have found that for special education to be included in the culture of the school district, a voice from special education must have a place at the leadership table. As we indicated in Chapter 6, a former superintendent of ours used to say, "We are not a system of schools; we are a school system," and consistency was always the goal. Curriculum, special education, bilingual education, grading, or homework—we strove for consistency, and to achieve this your voice needs to be heard. Your superintendent also needs to establish and reinforce your role with building principals.

What is your role in hiring, evaluating, supervision, and decision making relative to special education personnel? Site-based management often gives the building principal authority to hire and terminate all staff assigned to their school. Do you play any role in hiring special education personnel or, for that matter, in terminating special education personnel? Once special education staff are hired in a school, what is your role in evaluating their performance, and how is your input utilized when considering their possible termination? Supervision is another area for clarification; do you or the school principal supervise special education staff, and exactly how is that communicated to staff? Your superintendent plays a significant role in providing answers and direction for all of these issues. You must have a clear direct line of communication with the superintendent, and you must be on the same page when it comes to mission, vision, and goals for your department. Even when disagreements arise, having access to and the ability to communicate with your superintendent, regardless of the difficulties brought on by an issue, is essential.

Understanding the Superintendent's View

You need to establish early in your tenure the parameters of your relationship with the superintendent. What information do they want, and how often will you meet with them outside of the central office? Communication with your superintendent must be articulated—how often you meet, how much to keep them up-to-date on, and the various issues that you are confronting such as difficult cases, legal matters, budget needs, unanticipated expenses, staffing issues, supervisory concerns, future program development, and technology needs. In our experience over the years, we noticed some key areas that superintendents tended to focus on:

- Difficult cases.
- Ongoing awareness of budget items.
- Potential approaches to reducing expenditures.
- Individual building issues.
- Getting the "straight" scoop.
- Parent matters.
- Staffing issues.

We had an opportunity to ask a group of superintendents to indicate, in their view, high- and low-interest areas of special education. The results showed high interest in understanding each of the following:

- Legal requirements.
- Program development.
- Professional development related to special education.

On the flip side, the superintendents showed low interest in these areas:

- Individualized Education Plan (IEP) process.
- Disability identification.
- Transportation.

See Appendix VIII for the full results of our superintendent survey. Understanding what superintendents view as relevant to their overall involvement and understanding of special education will assist you as you work to provide your own superintendent with relevant information and data.

All of these considerations have a special education focus. If your role involves student services or pupil services, you may focus on guidance, nursing, Title I, or other areas that you will need to factor into your superintendent updates as well. Constantly comparing your district's information and data to those of surrounding or like districts as well as state data will put you in a better position when sharing information. We also found, through our experience, that our job as ASEs was to keep the superintendent informed, but not to get them involved, and we always came prepared with options and potential solutions. For a parent or staff matter, our goal was to keep the superintendent up-to-date by sharing those options and potential solutions, for example, but not asking for their involvement. In fact, we always felt the less the superintendent got involved, the better it served both the case and our ability to manage the case. When the superintendent got involved in contentious parent or staff matters that we had not previously brought to them, it never went well.

One such case involved a rejected IEP where the parent saw the superintendent at an evening meeting, and the superintendent made some commitments counter to the IEP Team's recommendations. The parent came to the office the next day to inform the ASE of the superintendent's commitment. Needless to say, this caused a great deal of concern that led to a conversation with the superintendent regarding the fallout and developing a strategy of how to deliver the message to the parents and the building IEP Team. Through these experiences, we established the rule that should the superintendent be faced with such circumstances in the future, they would advise the parent that they would discuss their concern with the ASE, and they would refrain from making any suggestions to parents, putting themselves in the middle of special education cases, in the future.

Establishing an honest relationship with your superintendent can be tricky for some. As with principals, establishing your interactions and expectations with your superintendent early on will prove productive. Just as we indicated with teachers being assigned a new paraprofessional and needing to establish expectations upfront and early, the same dynamic may exist with your superintendent. Your predecessor's relationship will remain current with your superintendent; the relationship may have been a positive one, and you will expected to keep it up. On the other hand, the relationship may have been less than positive, in which case you need to determine why and work to assure the superintendent that you are a Team player who wants to hear from them any and all concerns, just as you will keep them informed of significant matters. Developing trust takes time, but open and honest communication from day one will allow both of you to gain that trust.

Your relationship with the superintendent needs to be respectful, honest, and supportive with clear boundaries and expectations. You must be the decision maker, and the superintendent must support you and your decisions. You will be held accountable for the outcome of your decisions, but that goes with the role and inherent responsibility of the position.

The superintendent can and should be an advisor and confidant but leave the decision making to you regarding special education.

Sometimes you will be overruled because the superintendent has the final say, but that should be the exception to the practice, not the rule. Be sure to thoroughly think through your data, facts, options, and recommendations and prepare for any necessary discussion with the superintendent so that you can present all the facts and options depending on the focus of the discussion. Regardless of the superintendent's background or experience, you must present as the authority on special education. This thinking applies to other administrative positions within the district that you work with and/or report to when special education is a part of the discussion.

Assistant Superintendent

Depending on the organizational chart for your district, you may report to an assistant superintendent, you may hold that title in the district, or you may be at the assistant superintendent level. Whatever the structure, the assistant superintendent(s) can be an asset as well as an ally to you as the ASE. As with any administrative position in your district, you will need to cultivate an open and honest relationship in order to advance your mission, visions, and goals within the district. Addressing areas such as curriculum, assessment, Response to Intervention (RtI), professional development, data collection, and many others must be a joint working relationship. These positions, whether one or several, lend themselves to strengthening your position and your decision-making skills, contributing to district-wide discussion, and supporting any initiative that you put forth.

You must know the responsibilities of the assistant superintendent(s) and identify how they can assist you, and in turn how you can assist them. Aligning your issues and needs with theirs will strengthen both of your positions while benefiting the district. Each of us can remember turning to an assistant superintendent for advice and consultation, especially in the early years of our first positions as ASEs.

We often turned to the assistant superintendent(s) for assistance and advice on matters concerning personnel, whether related to staff performance and evaluation, overall supervision of department staff, contract-related issues, or a sounding board for thought. In later years of our tenure, the assistant superintendent(s) became partners in professional conversations regarding the quality of instruction, professional development, outcomes for students, report card formulation, student progress, literacy programs, utilization of general education support staff, and more. Wherever the assistant superintendent sits in relation to your position within the district, look at this position as one that can advance your mission for special education.

Business Manager

The recognized chief financial officer for the school district is a key player when it comes to the special education budget. Again, depending on the size of the district, one individual may take charge of the school finances, and several clerks may support the daily operation of the business office. In larger districts, an assistant or two may have decision-making authority. You may report to one of these positions, or if the district is large enough, you may have your own liaison to the business manager in your office. Whatever the organization structure calls for, you need to build a strong relationship—an open, honest, forthright, and collaborative relationship—with the business manager.

Given the enormity of special education costs, sometimes 20% to 25% of the school budget, the superintendent, the school committee, and the community pay much attention to the budget issue. You are responsible for keeping current on all aspects of the special education budget given the unanticipated expenditures that can and do occur in any school year. Your relationship with the business office must encourage openness and constant communication. Anticipated problems need to be stated and received with an attitude of "What can *we* do about it?," "What options are available to the district?," and so on.

You will require current data for all special education accounts, both for your department and for any school-based special education accounts. You also need current data related to any special education and other grants that you may oversee. You should have access to a monthly expenditure reporting system already in place, but if one does not exist, then work with your business office to develop a system that meets your overall needs. Current data allow you to keep the superintendent abreast of all account activities and those that may be trending toward a deficit. The business manager needs to collaborate with you on how the accounts are to be reported out so that projections can be made based on trends from previous years as well as the current school year. The special education budget is the most volatile area within the school budget. Numerous accounts can be impacted during the school year with unanticipated expenditures, so being on top and even ahead of this adverse impact to the budget can allow for time to make adjustments in the overall department and/or school budget to reduce the negative impact. The business manager is essential to this process, as in our collective experience they bring experienced solutions to a negative situation that we have no knowledge of.

You may need to educate the business manager on various requirements of the law and regulations, especially if they are new to the position. One approach that worked well for us with a new business manager when a student was recommended for an out-of-district placement was to schedule time to explain to the business manager the reason for the placement recommendation. This approach was effective in that the business manager began to gain an awareness of and appreciation for the need for an out-of-district tuition placement. The special education budget, as discussed with one town manager, is like the snow removal budget for the town; being in the black or red each year depends on the unpredictability of the weather.

Transportation

The individual responsible for transportation is another crucial position to connect yourself to. Again, the size of the district will determine where that individual sits—within your department, the business office, or a separate and distinct office, for example. Regardless of location, you need access to and a strong relationship with the transportation administrator, particularly when developing contracts on an annual basis or seeking to add new routes to the schools within the district. Complaints by parents, principals, private schools, and collaboratives can be the bane of your daily existence. You need to understand what is happening and who is responsible. Whether the district provides its own transportation, contracts the service to private vendors, or uses a combination of both, you need to know who is doing what and what is causing your problems, single or repetitive, and you need to fix them quickly. If your state requires vehicle inspections, you must be aware of the process, your district vehicles, and your contractors' vehicles.

Facilities

Whether school buildings come under the business office or a separate department within the district, a standing relationship with the facilities department is vital. In your position as ASE, on numerous occasions due to the specific needs of a student or group of students, you will need to take specialized action to accommodate those student needs. You may need to ask the facilities department to carpet a classroom, provide an air conditioner, install lighting or soundproofing, or create a separate space within a classroom. These accommodations will vary from year to year, but they will occur. Cultivating a positive ongoing relationship with the head of the facilities department will increase their awareness of and appreciation for the needs of a specific disability population or student so that they can better assist in providing the identified accommodations, which may include building a time-out area, a ramp, or a hanging sensory device; improving sound quality; or any other accommodation required for a given student, program, or general education classroom.

Special Education Instructional Space

Facilities and appropriate instructional space continue to be a struggle for many ASEs and school districts. Finding appropriate instructional space for special education instruction and services has long been an issue even with the construction of new school buildings. Space gets consumed quickly, and before long what once was desirable becomes less than. We have seen some remarkable creativity on the part of building administrators in providing space for special education programs and services. In working with building administrators, you can most times overcome obstacles to ensure provision of appropriate and adequate environments.

CHAPTER SUMMARY

Central office administrative positions can be and usually are the key to your success as an ASE. These professionals play both direct and indirect roles in the operation of your department, and their expectations and support are crucial to how the community perceives you as an administrator. You must cultivate this relationship so that trust in your judgment goes without question. Any initiative you seek will have a curriculum, budget, or staffing implication, and the ability to consult with your superintendent, assistant superintendent(s), and business manager to ensure they support your efforts will be critical. This may include involving the head of maintenance and building principals as you look for classroom space or perhaps a hanging device for sensory integration or carpeting for a class of students who are hearing-impaired. You must not shy away from developing these relationships; rather, embrace and cultivate them as the success of your efforts for your staff and students clearly depend on them.

Building Administrators 16

As mentioned throughout this book, principals, as well as administrators of special education (ASEs), have a difficult job, and each principal brings to the position their own leadership style and beliefs about serving students in special education. We hope your district values a well-informed group of building administrators led by a superintendent who supports inclusion for all students and the district's ability to respond to student needs within the general education classroom.

Relationship Building

We can relate dozens of anecdotal stories about building administrators supporting special education or being less supportive than we desired. While we may have experienced a lack of support in the early years of our career, ASEs can expect far less nowadays with the greater emphasis on inclusion and educating the whole child.

One principal had a student in a special education program at his school who had regularly occuring encopresis. So, he asked the parents to send in a change of clothes daily and often found himself assisting the student in the shower as well as changing his clothes. This went on for several weeks before the ASE learned of the situation, and when asked the principal responded that the program staff had a job to do in the classroom, and his job was to assist this student as needed. Contrast this with the principal who leaned on the ASE every time he was called into a classroom or program class to address a student as he felt it was not his job to address special education students; that was the ASE's job. Your goal is to establish a working relationship with all building administrators and, just as we suggest to teachers with their teaching assistants, establish the ground rules for your responsibilities and those of your principals. Most often this will involve personnel, parent, or student matters, but other issues to consider include fire drills, field trips, transportation concerns, decision-making responsibilities, supervision of special education personnel, program supervision and oversight, and more.

Building administrators come from varied backgrounds and experiences. Their own belief systems and values may vary somewhat from and therefore run counter to yours, which means that you need to negotiate the terrain of their school, to ensure that your programming is maintained and that your staff have what they require to achieve the expected outcomes for their students.

In the early years of special education reform, many principals did not have the experience or background to fully engage in the complexities of these new laws and requirements. For the most part, we found building administrators to be vested in doing what is best for children. But you may come across one or two whose field of understanding is not quite in line with yours. You will need to develop a strategy and make a concerted effort to establish a working relationship that will benefit your goals for the school as well as the principal's point of view. While you may feel the need to pull back or try to pull rank, that is a mistake. Instead, present your case with data and conviction that what you strive to do will benefit the school as a whole and the students within the school.

Site-Based Management

Understanding the dynamics of site-based management is essential to ensuring achievement of your initiatives in each building. Building principals, in our state of Massachusetts, have full control of their schools and, as discussed, sole authority over the hiring and termination of staff, including special education personnel. As the instructional leaders in their schools, they therefore have a significant say in how special education services are provided, particularly in general education classrooms. Your responsibility, as ASE, is to ensure implementation of students' Individualized Education Plans (IEPs) and provision of all required services. As indicated, each principal possesses their own leadership style and beliefs relative to special education provision. Some embrace inclusion, and others believe that special education services should be provided outside of the classroom.

Principals also oversee discipline, and ensuring that in considering students with special needs for suspension they are equipped to make decisions that do not put them or the district at risk of violating a student's rights is essential. We covered special education discipline in detail in Chapter 11, as many significant concerns can arise if individual students' rights are not specifically covered as indicated in the law(s). Principals also need to be aware of the requirements regarding student bullying and student restraint. Some principals want to leave these matters to the IEP Team and the special education staff, but they have a vested interest in ensuring that these matters are addressed in the most appropriate manner.

CHAPTER SUMMARY

Principals who agree with your belief system, mission, vision for the department will be a strong asset in the development of programs and services. They will see how to improve the overall standing of their school by working collaboratively with you and in turn for their students' outcomes. We should also point out that the principals who share your beliefs have already developed a culture that supports all students' learning in the Least Restrictive Environment (LRE). Like you, they made a commitment to professional development to enhance an inclusive culture. Remember that each principal has their own beliefs about special education services as well as inclusive services (inclusion). Developing an individual relationship with each principal will assist in your efforts to support your building staff and establish appropriate services for identified students.

We mentioned compensatory services, which principals need to understand and consider, and your need to ensure that students receive their required services. Currently, the COVID-19 pandemic is not viewed as an excuse to discontinue services, just as failing to find a service provider is inexcusable. Always be aware of your district's responsibility to provide compensatory services based on individual student or district issues that affect continuity of service(s) delivery as stated in the student's IEP. When situations do arise for providing compensatory service, be sure to address the student's needs in a responsible and timely manner.

17 Role of Various Special Education Personnel

Many new positions have arisen since the early years of the law such as behavioral specialist, Board Certified Behavior Analyst (BCBA), autism specialist, inclusion specialist, social worker, program supervisor, coordinator/Team chairperson, liaison, out-of-district coordinator, transition specialist, and vocational rehabilitation counselor. The role that each special education staff member plays needs to be clearly defined, in writing, and understood by all constituents. In our experience, special education personnel are often unable to articulate the role performed by various members of their own Team, and when that occurs, how can general education personnel be expected to know the roles of these positions? Titles do not always define a position, its responsibilities, and how it should function within the school. Titles need definition, along with roles and responsibilities. Keeping current on all job duties and descriptions will reduce confusion and ensure that all administrators and school-based staff as well as parents understand and appreciate the numerous positions within your department.

Special education personnel, building leaders, and general education staff may be unclear on what a position is intended to achieve. We have found that when new positions are added, all too often efforts have not been made to inform staff of the intended roles and responsibilities of these positions. In our view, failing to provide this clarity leads to assumptions about the role to play, which may conflict with the actual intent. Further, it forces the person in the role to not just explain what they do, but often defend their actions. Clearly, everyone needs to understand the expectations of each position.

Not only do these new positions need clarification; they also require a solid comprehensive job description to alleviate any assumptions staff might make. Throughout our careers, we made a point to focus on job descriptions as roles vary and change over time. Reviewing all job descriptions every few years allowed us to remain current with the performance of various staff and make any adjustments to ensure currency of the expectations for each position.

Some staff take on multiple roles—maybe due to staff shortages, maybe by design, maybe as part of the culture of the building. Whatever the reason, you as the administrator of special education (ASE) will need to fully understand the duality of and reasoning behind each role and strategize on ways to make the dual role more effective. We have found that individuals functioning in multiple roles are usually spread too thin to perform either role well.

Consultants may also provide services to students in your district, and eliminating any "assumptions" about their responsibilities and their work with students is important. ASEs must make every effort to ensure a full understanding by all constituents of their responsibilities and work with students.

CHAPTER SUMMARY

We have seen positions morph into something other than their original job description due to lack of supervision or to building administrators changing the responsibilities of the person in the position to suit the needs of the building without alerting the ASE. For these reasons, you must stay on top of the position's description to ensure that the individual fulfills appropriately the roles and responsibilities of the position. When roles are not clarified, others will shape them to fit their needs or the needs of the school.

18

Supervision and Evaluation of Department Staff

Supervision and evaluation of staff are topics of great significance for the special education department. As the administrator of special education (ASE), knowing who you are responsible to supervise and who you are responsible to evaluate is therefore important. Depending on your state, various regulations may apply to the supervision and evaluation of staff in your district. In our state, Massachusetts, site-based management gives building principals the authority to hire and terminate. If that is the case in your district, what is your responsibility in terms of overseeing staff at the school level? In his dissertation "Evaluating Special Education Teachers: Do We Get the Job Done?" Robert E. Widener Jr. (2011) indicated "that some administrators are adequately trained and some are not. Concerns were expressed that some administrators were satisfied with the performance of special education teachers and students as long as no behavior problems were present. Concern was expressed over the lack of training in special education during the principal preparation program at local colleges and universities. The suggestion was made that all administrators struggle with what a good evaluation looks like and the key, especially in a cotaught classroom, is to find a team that can and will work well together. Differentiated instruction may look different in each classroom. Finally, several of the school division participants reported that it was the perception that many administrators still did not take into account all additional responsibilities that are part of the special education teachers' job duties such as paperwork, alternative testing, and case management" (pp. 56–57).

Your staff in the schools walk a fine line, and your expectations or requirements of the law and regulations may put them at odds with what the school leadership requires or expects, so for you to remember that every day they must function as part of the school is vitally important. When conflict occurs, whom do staff turn to? Who is their supervisor—that is, must they show loyalty to the school principal or to you as the ASE? You must be aware of this dynamic and why establishing both supervisory and evaluative responsibilities is so important. When staff recognize that the principal who hired them also has the authority to terminate them, then you won't find it hard to guess where they'll direct their "loyalty." We spoke in Chapter 15 about strategies, and supervision and evaluation of department staff is one area that requires you to strategize.

The teacher's contract may spell out the details of the performance evaluation at the building level and your role, or lack thereof, in the process. Regardless of your defined role and responsibilities as either a direct or contributing evaluator, you need to clearly understand the principal's expectations. Principals may present with strong evaluation skills as applied to general education teachers, but their skills may not be so strong when it comes to special education personnel. Whether they acknowledge that or not, your responsibility is to support building principals and your staff when necessary. You can review the principal's previous evaluation of your staff to get a sense of their skill level if you are new to the district. Should you have extensive experience in the district, then you may already be aware of the principal's skill level.

When we started out in this field of special education, we had to conduct the evaluation of our staff. As our departments grew in number, many of us were able to shift the primary responsibility of evaluating special education teachers to the principals while we kept the specialists, itinerant staff, and for some of us the nurses. As time evolved, our role morphed into more of a contributing one that entailed signing off on the principal's evaluation. Whatever system your district puts in place, you must engage with the primary evaluator in order to contribute positive information and raise your concerns about their performance should any exist.

One aspect of supervision and evaluation to keep in mind is that you cannot evaluate all the staff in your department. Your position is too cumbersome to allow for even *thinking* of conducting observation and evaluation of all department staff. If responsibility is not shared with building administrators, it should be. Do not get caught in a system whereby you are required to perform all the evaluations. Be sure that you fully understand the requirements before accepting the position and once in the position attempt to reduce your workload of supervision and evaluation depending on the size of the district.

With respect to retaining new staff, as one assistant superintendent related to one of us, when in doubt about a staff member's capability to perform the responsibilities of the position, or if you are not sure of their potential, do not keep them on staff, especially after two years. Do not make the mistake of allowing a mediocre staff member to remain on the Team; their poor performance will affect the operation of the program, classroom instruction, the service that they are providing, and the progress of the students. This applies to any position within your department. One of us got a call from a principal, one day, informing us that they did not want to return a first-year teacher. This principal as the primary evaluator was responsible for meeting the appropriate requirements for the staff member's formal evaluation. Asked if all required documentation was in place, the principal informed us that the final observation and consultation had not been completed. Failing to complete this final piece of the evaluation meant that the staff member would be extended a contract for the following school year and could not be terminated. All involved agreed that we would complete the final observation and consultation and together with the principal develop an improvement plan for the staff member. This experience led to working with the superintendent's leadership group (to which we belonged) to develop a process for the principal to reach out to ensure that we attended to any staff member who they believed was not performing up to standard.

Making consistent practice of conducting school walk-throughs will provide you with a sense of who is—and who is not—providing quality classroom instruction. You can follow up with more frequent visits to these classrooms and discuss your concerns with the principal. This will enable you to be part of the solution rather than playing catch-up later in the process. If any staff members in your department are ineffective or unable to perform the required tasks of the position, you can take the necessary steps to improve their situation or make the required personnel changes. Too much is at stake for students to risk maintaining ineffective personnel, especially when it comes to direct service providers.

In Chapter 3, we discussed the importance of developing a relationship with the teacher's union—an idea that came to us in a rather unique way. One day, while visiting teachers during a walk-through of a school, one of us was very surprised to enter a special education classroom and observe a teacher sitting behind a desk, reading a newspaper, and the students doing as they pleased. Asked what they were doing, the teacher's response was first "reading the paper" and then, after further inquiry into what the students were doing, "I'm not sure; I haven't finished reading the paper yet." After leaving the room, the one of us who experienced this visited the principal, whose advice was to speak to the superintendent. The superintendent, however, advised in favor of bringing the matter to the union, and though this response was peculiar, we decided to inform the union president of our observation and resulting belief in the need for some form of discipline. "Let me understand this," the president answered. "You were in the classroom once, and you *think* that some form of discipline is in order. Well, tell me, what have you done to assist the teacher to improve their practices? Before you impose any discipline, you will have to come to me with a file drawer full of efforts you have put forth to assist the teacher in their performance." He then asked, "Who sent you to me?"

It turned out that the district had attempted to terminate the teacher on at least two previous occasions and failed. The union president then asked, "Can we go off the record?," and proceeded to disclose that our observations likely were not wrong, but the district likely never took the time to put together that file drawer. He ended the conversation by advising that if we ever had an issue that might make its way back to the union, we were free to inform him (not to have him change our actions) simply to avoid blindsiding the union. Remember, it always works better to share potential actions, even when disagreements have occurred. We kept this experience in mind throughout our careers, even when we anticipated a challenging situation ahead. We also made it a point to seek out the union leadership of every district we served to share our practice of keeping them informed.

CHAPTER SUMMARY

Supervision and evaluation of your staff is one of the ASE's most significant responsibilities. The staff that you hire, supervise, and evaluate can make or break your program and service options. Whether you serve as primary or contributing evaluator, you must understand the requirements of the teacher's contract in your district, along with any state requirements, and be attentive to the work of your staff to ensure continuous quality of instruction. Ensuring that department staff fulfill the requirements and responsibilities of their position with respect to all aspects of the position is essential. These individuals are charged with providing special education services to students, and you need to be confident in their capacity to fulfill this important role. The clearer you and school principals are on your roles in evaluation and supervision of special education personnel, the more comfortable each of you will become, but more importantly, the more comfortable staff will be in expanding their skills and seeking support when indicated.

Your staff certainly must know the expectations of the law and regulations and, in turn, your established expectations. They need to hear from you that if school leadership requires them to take an action against your established expectations, they need to inform you, and you then need to take the lead in working with leadership regarding the rationale for these expectations. As indicated, all school leaders have their own set of expectations and their own style of leading. Your job, or your designee's job, is to work with each of them individually, educating them on special education requirements and reminding them that staff are simply working to ensure compliance.

Budget Development 19

Budget may be an area in which you have little or no experience. If that is the case, reach out to colleagues in neighboring districts; after all, they were once similarly inexperienced at some point in their tenure and as such will be more than willing to assist. Ask your business manager how they would like you to share budget-related information and what they expect to see for rationale and data in your budget request. You need to develop a good understanding of your superintendent's, and ultimately your school committee's, expectations. The district will use a formatted process for budget submission and presentation, whether it is department-based, school-based, or in the case of special education a combination of school- and department-based through the various special education programs. Whatever the existing approach, the initial budget you submit for your department must include everything you envision for the next school year. As the process continues, knowing that you have submitted a comprehensive budget will become even more significant if you are asked to make "cuts" from the budget you submitted.

Unanticipated Expenditures

You also never want to find yourself in a position where some expenditure arises that you discover you did not include in the budget. Clearly, tuition, transportation, and legal costs may all go beyond what you budgeted for the school year. When these unanticipated expenditures arise, move them forward to the superintendent and business office as soon as possible to put in place any necessary corrective actions, which may include notification to the school committee and town government.

Budget Consumption

Many new and even veteran administrators of special education (ASEs) struggle with budget. Our experience has shown that those who have taken a graduate class in budgeting commonly respond that it did not prepare them for the complexities of assessing needed information, particularly from staff and others. Nor did such a course inform them how to proceed when defending new requests or how to utilize data to support these requests. Putting together an annual budget takes time, and we have heard many ASEs indicate that this time commitment takes away from the "important" aspects of their work. Your budget is yet another necessary evil, but also a tool that can define your mission, vision, and goals for your department and the district. The more detail you can assemble to support your request for additional funds or additional staff, the better the outcome may be.

Far too often, we have seen ASEs publicly evaluated on their tuition and transportation budgets. Special education likely covers anywhere from 20% to 25% of your school district's entire budget, and the public and many in your district are not aware that special education laws are entitlement laws, which means that students must be served regardless of cost. In our state of Massachusetts, when a student ages out of special education (turning 22 years of age), they may receive services from a human resource agency at the state level. The funding for these state agencies is not an entitlement; rather, it is "contingent upon appropriation." You and your school district, however, do not have that language or luxury, instead having "entitled to a Free and Appropriate Public Education (FAPE)" regardless of cost. We know that some placements are very costly when a student requires services beyond what you can offer within the district, and when you add transportation into the equation, the already high cost becomes even more so.

Program development therefore becomes an important consideration prior to budget time each year. When we took on the ASE position back in the 1970s, special education was a priority reimbursement at the state level, and school districts received 110% of expenditures by the prototypes mentioned earlier, based on the formula developed at the state level. Needless to say, that did not last long, as many districts began including in their Individualized Educaton Plans (IEPs) services such as guidance and reading that were not authorized as special education expenditures, and we found ourselves spending a good deal of our efforts not only developing a budget but monitoring expenditures throughout the school year. As new ASEs, we had not been trained for this, nor had we contemplated budgeting when we accepted the position. We know that in our state the average percentage of a school district's budget allocated to special education over the past several years has exceeded 21%, and we also know that many people still question these expenditures, which can be exceedingly high. We spoke in Chapter 9 of the need to continually assess student needs and develop programs to meet those needs. Annual assessment of all students serviced outside of the district to determine if a program can be put in place to return them to the district is a clear priority. Knowing how your state makes services available for students receiving a special education, particularly if they require these services in a residential setting, is equally important.

A significant portion of most districts' budgets are allocated to staffing, and you will very likely need to defend these positions annually by showing their impact on student learning and development. Budget is an aspect of your job where the five *P*s—Prior Preparation Prevents Poor Performance—are critical. You need to approach a budget meeting anticipating any questions that might arise and arriving prepared with the data to back up what you are requesting and looking to defend. For new requests in the budget or requesting an increase to a line item, be prepared not only to show the need and cost benefit to your strategy for the request, but also to respond when asked what you will "cut" to offset your requests. If you cannot provide an answer to this question, then demonstrate the need for and long-term cost benefit to the additional request. As a strong suggestion, do not indicate that special education is an entitlement, or that the school committee has to fund your request. Use data showing cost benefit over the long term to demonstrate the positive impact of the request for new funds to support the initiative.

In some years you may seek additional staff, and in other years your focus may be additional contracted services, instructional materials, assessment tools, equipment, or the never-ending need for staff and student technology. Whatever you might be seeking, prepare yourself to defend the request. Always plan a well-thought-out justification for any new request and include illustrated comparison data in support of your request; if the district does not fund it, what will happen?

As we noted in Chapter 9, identifying three students with a particular need is the general rule to develop a program, and a comprehensive review of students placed outside of your district, along with staff knowledge regarding potential students in need of a specific program, will allow you to determine if you have a sufficient population of students. Defense of a budget can initially be a daunting task. You must first gather the necessary information to assemble the overall budget, then defend it to the superintendent and in some districts to the entire leadership Team, and finally defend it to the school committee and again in some districts to the town government. Our approach each year was to present an initial budget that contained everything that we believed the department required; rather than anticipating what might not be accepted, we waited to be told that a request was rejected. We never wanted to hear someone asking why we did not include a provision in our budget. We built our budgets based on what we knew and always utilized current data to support our requests.

Your state may have a financial offset for tuitions and transportation costs similar to our state. The Massachusetts "Circuit Breaker" reimburses school districts for all costs beyond three times the established per-pupil cost for the school year, referred to as foundation, at up to 75% depending on the amount budgeted by the legislature. Some school districts budget a contingency amount to cover unanticipated special education costs, although we have seen this option used in only a limited number of districts. Years ago, we learned of a district where several students moved in requiring placements in an out-of-district program for students on the autism spectrum. The ASE notified the superintendent and in turn the school committee. The superintendent determined after educating the school committee on the fiscal implications of students moving into the district that the same type of educational awareness should be made available to the town fathers (select board members, city or town counsel members, mayors, managers, etc.) as he wanted everyone to understand that this was not a reflection of the school district's ability to service special education students or to budget appropriately, but a requirement of the law that the new district replicate all services the students were receiving in their IEPs in the previous district. This example also shows the strong bond between the superintendent and the ASE, particularly in supporting the need for all involved to understand the complexities of the law and its regulations.

Our state has since changed the language related to the date that a district becomes responsible for students who move in, but some districts still grapple with providing a contingency for unanticipated placements, from within the district, in their budget.

Special education grant funds will also have an important effect on your budget. In relation to your receipt of federal funds, be aware that the Individuals With Disabilities Education Act (IDEA) requires that students with disabilities, from your district, who are parentally placed in private schools and in need of special education and related services be identified, located, evaluated, and provided such services consistent with the requirements. Your district must have a full understanding of policies and procedures for calculating the proportionate share for these students that your state has in place. In recent years, our state was required to respond to complaints, which led to the provision of training and enhanced the significance for local ASEs as they went about determining how to calculate and administer these students' proportionate share. Under 34 C.F.R. § 300.133(a), each Local Education Agency (LEA) must spend a proportionate amount of IDEA Part B funds on providing special education and related services (including direct services) to parentally placed private school children with disabilities. The regulations specify that the LEA makes the final decisions about the services provided to eligible parentally placed private school children with disabilities, based in part on input provided through the consultation process by appropriate private school representatives and representatives of parents of these particular students. Fully understanding how your federal funds must be allocated to cover your responsibilities with proportionate share is important and likely to be looked at when your state is conducting compliance monitoring in your district.

Maintenance of effort (MOE), another requirement of IDEA, stipulates that an LEA may not reduce the amount of local, or state and local, funds spent for the education of children with disabilities below the amount spent for the preceding fiscal year. If a district included positions as a part of their local budget that they wanted to fund the next school year with grant funds, and proposed the local funds that had previously supported the special education positions be utilized for general education expenditures, they would not be maintaining their effort to support special education. Under IDEA Part B, funds provided to an LEA must be used to supplement, not supplant, state, local, and other federal funds. This can be hard for some administrators and school committee members to understand, particularly when available budgets are being tightened.

Staff Engagement

As you develop your budget, involve your staff in the process. You may use a form, or need to develop one, that asks each of them to outline their needs for the upcoming school year, as you never want to find yourself faced with a staff member saying that you never asked them what they require to do their job. This should also include an assessment of professional development needs so that you are prepared to establish an amount for this as well. The amount of federal grant monies that your district receives for special education can assist you with addressing some of the costs mentioned; however, remember that these monies are specifically intended for expansion of service options. We have found that in recent years, many superintendents have begun to utilize these grant monies to move personnel off the local budget. This can pose a significant problem with a district's MOE, which requires school districts to ensure consistency in spending on special education. Using grant funding in this manner can also be viewed as supplanting, or utilizing federal grant monies to offset local budget allocations, which is prohibited. An example would be removing several staff positions from the local budget and covering those costs with federal grant funds. Your business office and superintendent may want you to do this to lessen special education costs in the local budget, and you must educate them on the aspects of MOE and supplanting to ensure the district is not put in jeopardy.

Your job is to make sure this is understood and that these grant funds are utilized to enhance services, not to displace expenditures in the local budget. When finances get tight, this often becomes a concern, and your school committee or town government may pressure the use of federal funds to offset local expenditures; they too will require education relative to the requirements and the potential risk to the district. Many states have seen initiatives similar to Proposition 2½ in our state, which legislatively restricts spending to no more than 2.5% percent of previous-year spending. These limits on overall spending make it difficult for some districts to provide internal services, resulting in placement of students outside of the district at significant costs. With the costs related to special education and the requirement of the entitlement regardless of cost, the better informed your school committee and local town government is relative to this dynamic, the more likely they will be to maintain services and programs within the district and continue to uphold their fiscal posture with special education requirements.

Medicaid

Medicaid reimbursement is another consideration when developing your budget. Your staff invest time into these claims, and likely someone in your office is responsible to coordinate this effort throughout the school year. As you go about defending your budget, share these efforts as well as the fact that you cannot access this option without explicit parent permission, which often takes time to assure the parents of the validity of the request. It is also important to share that in 2019 Medicaid reimbursement was expanded to include 504 services, individual health care plans, and other medically necessary services, and this only expanded the time and staff involved in the process.

CHAPTER SUMMARY

Budgeting for special education can be a volatile experience for any ASE. Unanticipated expenditures, a single residential placement, a hearing decision where the parents prevailed, a move in a case, a settlement—all add to an already weighty budget. For some, the presentation of the special education budget is an arduous experience. Backing up your request with solid data will provide you with the defensive language needed to justify and support your position. The budget is the lifeline for special education, and you must formulate it based on what you know, as well as what your department requires, and support your requests with accurate and comprehensive data. Always be prepared to share with all department members and involve them in decisions with which you choose to move forward. The last thing you want to hear from staff or a principal is "You never sought our input."

As indicated in this chapter, you and your department are often judged based on your budget. Transportation, tuition, and staffing costs are the focus of your superintendent, school committee, and town fathers. You may have solid programming, extensive professional development for your staff, and full compliance, but if you go over your budget, no one will be asking about these achievements. Instead, everyone will be asking you to explain *why*! Your special education budget is often a "best guess" of your expectations for the upcoming year, yet as we

(Continued)

must emphasize, the situation can change very quickly. Your relationship with your business office is critical in ensuring that no one gets surprised, and the main reason for your place at the leadership table is to provide everyone with a full understanding of when special education finances become a focus.

PART IV

Extraordinary Concerns

20 Dealing With Difficult Cases

How do you go about determining a case may be difficult? From our standpoint, once again, it begins with listening. A staff member, a principal, a parent, a community representative, or a human service provider may share something that you, as the administrator of special education (ASE), need to follow up on. Always keep in mind that small things often harvest into larger things that can sting you later. When information is shared with you, always give it attention. If a parent shares a concern, speak to the teacher(s) or staff member(s) who have the required information. As you visit classrooms, always ask staff to make you aware of any situations of concern with a case, a family, or a child. Throughout this book we have emphasized your role in supporting staff, and dealing with difficult cases is an area of significance. Working with students is a difficult job, and when a situation takes on an added dimension, you must ensure that your staff can continue their work without distraction. When differences occur over a student's progress, parents and others often look to target the staff member. We always felt our role was to intervene and let the individual see us, not the staff member, as the one raising the concern. The more we took on the position of "flack catcher," the less the staff member needed to shoulder the negativity.

Do not allow a case or situation to get out of control, or it will control you—and it won't take much. One of the quickest ways to lose control of a case is to ignore it or fail to respond in a timely manner. You cannot avoid the situation indefinitely, so why put it off? The longer you wait, the more difficult and complicated the case will become, especially when the complainant takes the issue to your supervisor before you have a chance to respond. Be upfront and honest from the get-go and address each and all concerns in a personal and professional manner. Strategize by using the resources around you—other administrators, staff in whom you place great trust, out-of-district colleagues with whom you have a standing relationship. No resource is too insignificant when dealing with a difficult case. Your objective is to resolve the difficult case to a reasonable satisfactory conclusion where both parties accept the outcome.

Due process hearings are an incredibly stressful experience for everyone involved, with the exception of the attorneys. The decision to proceed to a hearing requires great thought and planning. Hearing decisions in our state of Massachusetts have historically turned out 50% in favor of parents and 50% in favor of the school district. So, if you think you have a very solid case, remind yourself of a few things before proceeding. None of your staff has ever been trained as a witness. They may be incredibly good at what they do, but being cross-examined by an attorney is not a skill they ever thought would be a part of their job description. After one hearing that lasted eight days over several weeks, a highly trained and experienced speech/language therapist resigned from her position and did not return to the field of education, reasoning that the entire hearing process was too trying and stressful for her to continue. This may be an extreme example of the impact of the hearing process on staff, but the reality is the process will affect your staff, whether they work in a general or special education capacity.

Should you proceed to a hearing, the staff involved will be away from their students for several days; the average hearing in our state, for example, lasts three to five days, and that does not account for preparation time with your attorney prior to the hearing. Again, at best you have a 50% chance of prevailing. Notice we did not say *winning*. One side or the other, the parents or the district, will see the hearing officer make a judgment that goes in their favor. Choosing not to view hearings in terms of wins and losses, we always recognized that one side prevailed and that ultimately the hearing officer found the best outcome for the student. Both of us know ASEs who proceeded to a hearing when a student's parents disagreed with their recommendations for the student, and in our experience when an ASE has developed a program to service students with similar needs and cannot understand why a parent will not agree to send their child to the program, these ASEs see only a win or a loss. As we indicated in Chapter 3, if you focus on the students' needs, you cannot make a wrong move, and this goes for due process as well: The hearing officer will determine the best services and placement for the student. Yes, you have options beyond a hearing, such as appealing to the courts; however, in only a very few cases has a school district "won" via appeal. An attorney enlightened us years ago by reminding us that we served students until they graduated or turned 22, which could amount to many years if the student student started receiving services in preschool or elementary school. The student's parents would be included in all meetings and decisions moving forward, so making well-informed decisions before advancing toward a hearing, and potentially beyond, best serves the student as well as the district.

One aspect of the job that we needed to learn was how to engage in the difficult conversations—the ones that you know you need to initiate, that keep you up at night. Whether with a parent, staff member, principal, superintendent, school committee member, town father, or student, these conversations require a great deal of thought, and in many instances practice, before they occur. Years ago, as noted in previous chapters, we were advised to wait 24 hours before reacting to a significant matter, such as a letter, an email, a text, or negative information otherwise brought to our attention. The advice was always to compose our response but wait 24 hours before sending it. The same advice applies to difficult conversations. Keep in mind that your response, if given in the heat of the moment, may have unexpected negative implications. Taking the time to record your thoughts and wait allows you not only to revisit your initial reaction and determine if it is still appropriate but also to consider the ramifications of your response.

In their book *Difficult Conversations*, Douglas Stone, Bruce Patton, and Sheila Heen (2000) provide many examples of conversations in which one party or another misinterprets what they hear. Stone et al. indicate that "blame is always about judgement and always looks back" (p. 60); you should always endeavor to move forward and refrain from assigning blame (looking back). Another book that contains many good lessons is *Getting to Yes*, in which Roger Fisher and William Ury (1981) share strategies for conflict resolution and for negotiating without compromise. Much of your job, as we have indicated, involves strategizing and bringing about resolution. Whether you are dealing with parents, staff, fellow administrators, or anyone else with whom you are required to interact, your goal must always be to find a way to "get to yes."

CHAPTER SUMMARY

Difficult cases will inevitably appear throughout the school year. Your goal should be to reduce the number of difficult cases and the frequency by which they occur. To do that, you need to put in place effective management strategies and practices that will ensure effective communication among staff and across schools with both staff and parents. Training staff to recognize when a case may become problematic and providing follow-up as to why and what they could have done to prevent it from rising to a level of difficulty must be a part of any processes and training you develop. Staying on top of the problem and responding in a timely manner will assist in defusing the situation. Difficult cases will always occur; the challenge is to minimize the chance of these cases absorbing valuable hours of your time. To do this, you need to establish effective strategies for communication and defensible programs and services. One tip is to prevent surprises to parents. You never want to hear a parent say, "This is the first time I have heard this" or "Why wasn't I told of this sooner?" or even "What do you mean my child cannot read at the fourth-grade level?" These types of responses from parents are an indicator of closed communication lines—school and home communication are out of sync. Staff need to know what to expect when a case begins to simmer, including the steps they should follow to keep the case from becoming difficult. This process is crucial to the success you will experience in minimizing difficult cases on an annual basis as well as for the long term. Enabling staff to recognize a problem, including how to approach it from the very beginning, whom to share the information with, and how to proceed within the district or department, is essential. In developing startegies, use your own thoughts, training, and experiences, but those of your staff as well. What do they think is a good strategy or the best way to proceed? What worked for them in the past? Seek out an administrator or colleague from whom you know you will get sound advice. Don't feel you have to go it alone. The important takeaway is that you develop strategies to deal with difficult cases.

21 Advocates

Our state of Massachusetts has a long history of advocacy by special interest groups for how special education operates at the state and local level. Advocates, their associations, and the interests of other parties can influence the actions a district may undertake to maintain and develop quality programs and services.

These influences can also create an environment at the local level where cost-benefit decisions are not necessarily made in the best interest of a student, but determined by the parents' beliefs about what is best for the student. A conflict may arise that can only be resolved through mediation, a hearing, or, in some cases, a settlement.

Advocates may appear to be a necessary evil, but the underlying concern for you as the administrator of special education (ASE) is why parents feel that they need one. For example:

- They felt negatively about previous experiences with the special education department.
- They perceived the information that they received about their child as negative.
- Other parents within their child's classroom or others within your district shared "horror stories" about their experience with special education.

A parent may secure the services of an advocate for a multitude of reasons. Many parents see the entire special education process as stressful; rejecting an Individualized Education Plan (IEP) and dealing with a state agency, for example, just takes their stress and anxiety to another level. Having someone to assist them through this process can be very welcoming. We sometimes took the approach of inviting parents from the Special Education Parent Advisory Council (SEPAC) to counsel other parents in understanding the entire special education process. This strategy worked well, especially with supportive members from the SEPAC.

Our state has many public and private agencies as well as individual advocates and attorneys who specialize in the special education appeal process. Most important for you as the ASE is to accept that advocates exist and that you will have to develop strategies to work together. Some advocates are extremely professional and want to serve in children's best interests. Others may have a torch to carry for their own personal reasons or due to experience with other school districts. Again, you will have to find ways to work with these advocates regardless of how difficult it may seem. The goal is to allow your staff to continue to do their work without getting involved in the potential demands of an advocate. *You need to act as the buffer between the advocate and your staff.* Obviously, depending on the size of your district, other middle managers, supervisors, or coordinators may be responsible for dealing with advocates. Team chairpersons or assistant principals may officially interact with the advocates, but you too must do whatever is required to ensure that your staff are not distracted by interaction with advocates. Training for staff is essential to their ability to deal effectively with advocates, attorneys, and parents who may be difficult and demanding.

Should you work with an advocate who specializes in a disability category that you may not feel confident in, secure the needed professional to assist you in dealing with the advocate, the family, and the case. Do not hesitate to reach out to that specialist, whether on staff or as a consultant, for the expertise to assist you in handling the case and potential ramifications. When not sure, look for the assistance that you may need. Your level of awareness in all disability categories will vary, so be willing to acknowledge this and access the necessary assistance to be effective in your position and produce results that are reasonable and satisfactory to all parties. In our careers as ASEs, we relied on consultants to assist us in our weaker areas. Because of this action, we became more knowledgeable about and confident in working with advocates in both general and specific cases.

You need to establish a written policy for how staff work with advocates, attorneys, or other interested parties a parent may bring to a Team meeting for support. Any guidelines that your state department of education has established, along with what is codified in laws and regulations for these individuals both at Team meetings in the schools and in outside environments, need to be a part of the policy you put in place. We developed what we called Decorum Standards for Special Education Team Meetings and Special Conferences (Appendix IX). Over time, this tool became useful for assisting staff to reduce certain types of inappropriate behavior by advocates, independent evaluators, and friends of parents at Team meetings. Such standards also help school-based staff gain confidence in their position as Team members who expect to be treated with respect and professionalism.

CHAPTER SUMMARY

The roles and responsibilities of advocates do not follow consistent practice or guidelines. Parents are allowed to bring someone to meetings to assist them, and often they invite an advocate. Because our state offers no certification or licensure to become an advocate, the role can be solely determined by the individual who is serving in this role. Your job is to find a way to work with the advocate and to do so in a professional manner. As always, you want to protect your staff, prepare them to work with parent representatives, and take whatever action might be required in the event of a less-than-positive interaction.

You can avoid the pitfalls, in one way by not avoiding advocates. Because you will eventually have to deal with them, it's better to do so on your terms than on theirs.

- Know the case that an advocate is engaged in.

- Know the issues.

- Clarify with staff.

- Don't hesitate to talk with the parent(s).

- Be sure you understand their grievance; work with them.

- Should the communication and requests become unreasonable, offer mediation, and use it as a proactive tool.

Seek opportunities to work productively with parents even if communication must go through their advocate, regardless of how difficult it may seem. As the ASE for the district, you have a reputation of accessibility, reasonableness, and thoughtfulness to uphold, and your primary goal is always to do the best for students.

22

Due Process, Appeal Hearings, and Mediation

Several areas of the law are rather "boilerplate," and this includes due process, appeal hearings, and mediation along with Section 504, age of majority, and disciplining students with special needs. We believe that although they are straightforward, they are worthy of review.

Due Process

When a dispute occurs between a student's parents and the school district with regard to the services recommended for the student in their Individualized Education Plan (IEP), the parents have a right to resolve the dispute through a third party. In our state, Chapter 30A of the Massachusetts General Laws governs due process proceedings. Your state may have a different due process requirement, but we will focus on the process as outlined in Massachusetts. Once an IEP has been rejected in our state, it must be sent to the Bureau of Special Education Appeals (BSEA) within five days of rejection. (Keep in mind that your state may follow a different process, and we advise you to become familiar with the due process proceedings and rules for your state.) Then, within 15 days, the school district must set a date for a resolution meeting with the rejecting party to see if the two sides can find a way to reach an agreement. A hearing cannot be held in response to a parent's request until a resolution meeting is held, both parties agree to mediation, or both parties waive the resolution meeting. When a resolution meeting is held, it must include the student's parent(s), relevant members of student's IEP Team, and a school representative with decision-making authority to attempt to resolve the issue(s) in the hearing request. Should the resolution meeting not prove successful, then the parties can move on to mediation or ultimately a due process hearing. While this process is under consideration, the school district *must* remember the five-day rule, which stipulates that copies of all documents to be introduced (exhibits) and a list of all witnesses to be called at the hearing must be received by the opposing party (or parties) and the hearing officer at least five business days prior to the hearing unless otherwise allowed by the hearing officer. We know of districts that set a hearing date but did not meet the five-day rule, which meant they were unable to introduce their exhibits or have their witnesses heard. We point this out as a word of technical compliance advice.

The same five-day rule will apply should a prehearing conference be held. This may occur when clarification is required or to simplify the issues as well as review the possibility of settling the case. Not every case will require a prehearing conference. If the issues are clear, a case may proceed directly to hearing.

For example, we might think our program and IEP offerings clearly fit a particular student, and then we would remember to consider how long the student would remain the school district's responsibility. As we indicated in Chapter 20, should the student happen to enter the district as a preschooler, we were looking at potentially another 18 years of working with the student and their family. We would be reminded that for parents seeking placement outside of the district, it would require not simply a one-year cost but rather multiyear costs; if the placement cost $50,000–$60,000 and the student remained there for several years, for example, the placement could potentially exceed $200,000–$400,000. In our view, every case was a potential multiple-thousand-dollar investment.

Seeking Solid Counsel

On numerous occasions, you will need legal representation. Throughout the school year, a variety of issues will arise that you cannot resolve on your own. Realizing this upfront can prevent costly mistakes, regardless of whether they affect your daily practice, a mediation session, a resolution session, a special education discipline issue, or a hearing. Whether you work in a small rural district, a suburban district, or a large urban district, situations will arise in which you need to rely on competent legal counsel to assist you in navigating the complex issues that you encounter.

Should you be new to a district and not yet fully briefed on (or not yet sure) which cases may be difficult, talk to the district's legal representation (should one be in place), including Team chairpersons, program coordinators, school psychologists, and/or building principals. These individuals should have the background information that you need to proceed to a satisfactory conclusion.

As indicated in the previous section, due process can be overly complex, and it is very significant that you access an attorney who specializes in special education law. The first hearing for one of us featured representation by the city's attorney who admitted to knowing nothing of special education due process. That meant writing out questions to ask various witnesses and handing them to her. After the initial hearing, she asked if we could write the briefs as well. The good news came when we received an invitation to the mayor's office where the same attorney, also in the office, proceeded to inform the mayor that special education litigation was very technical, it would take her years to become well enough informed to represent the school district, and the city owed it to the school district to secure an attorney who could provide comprehensive and knowledgeable counsel. With that, we gained the ability to access the best attorneys available—Richard Sullivan, Esq., and Thomas Nuttall, Esq.—who actually represented both of us, as it turned out, for the remainder of our careers. You need to develop a trusting relationship with your attorney. We recall a few colleagues who hesitated to run issues by their attorney as they feared the attorney would place blame or challenge their position, but your attorney, as your ally, must always believe that any situation can be worked with.

When disputes or differences occur, it can be difficult for one side to see the other side's position. In seeking solid counsel, we often get caught up in the facts of the case, believing that we know what the student requires and even that our recommended services are "the best." We always relied on our attorneys to keep the situations that arose in our careers in proper perspective. So when, as the administrator of special education (ASE), do you know that you need an attorney? In most instances, you should be able to attend meetings without an attorney even when a student's parents bring one. Resolving differences relating to a student's IEP, though challenging, does not necessarily require significant legal advice. We both remember the feeling of being in a room with parents and attorneys and having to potentially make decisions that were counter to the IEP Team's recommendations for the student. Many of these meetings did not require an attorney to attend; in such situations, however, you need to ensure coverage of all legal requirements. When these situations arose for us, we would contact our attorneys to prepare for entering the meeting, and they would remind us of the realities of the situation from both a financial and a personal standpoint. We have continued to indicate the importance of the five *P*s—Prior Preparation Prevents Poor Performance— and entering a meeting where there is potential for challenge to the district's offer requires you to know what you will agree to and when you need to walk away. Enlisting an attorney who knows what you are offering in terms of programs or services will allow you to assess the situation and know when you should move forward to defend your offerings for the student. Should you arrive at a Team meeting and the parents have legal representation, you have options: adjourn the meeting until you can have your own legal representation; proceed with the Team meeting with the understanding that the parents' attorney cannot participate, but can observe, or proceed with the Team meeting based on your level of confidence about the issues and your ability to bring resolution to the case.

Should you proceed to a hearing, your attorney will know what evidence you have, who you will call as witnesses, and what it will take to inform the hearing officer that the school district's recommendation for the student was right. The evidence put forward, by both parties, will be what the hearing officer considers in making a decision.

Placement costs are not the only financial matter to consider; hearing costs are a factor as well. Depending on the attorneys' costs in your area, which for most districts in our state run on average $200–$250 per hour, you need to consider prep time for your witnesses, discovery time for your attorney to gather evidential information, time on the record at the hearing, and time for any potential legal briefs or summaries that the hearing officer needs before rendering a decision. The hours can and do add up; if prep takes one day, discovery takes one day, the hearing takes three days, and after-hearing time takes one day, you are potentially looking at the cost for your attorney in the area of $10,000 minimum. Still another factor to consider is the potential costs of the parents' attorneys should the district not prevail at the hearing. Our attorneys always told us to anticipate the cost related to the parents' attorney to be double the district's hourly rate. Because the parents' attorney was entitled to "a reasonable rate" of the prevailing costs, that meant charging in the vicinity of $20,000 at a minimum. You must discuss all these financial matters with your attorney as you consider moving a rejected IEP forward to a hearing. Your state may employ a different due process proceeding than our state, and your expenses may be far less; even so, some costs merit consideration as you determine how to proceed.

One of us saw an IEP rejected when the parents were seeking a private special education school. We felt that the program offered in the IEP was the right one for the student in addition to meeting the Free and Appropriate Public Education (FAPE) and Least Restrictive Environment (LRE) requirements. After conferring with our attorney, we offered the parents the average per-pupil cost if they chose to send their child to the special education school. Our attorney fully understood that we believed our IEP was appropriate; however, he reminded us of the cost of moving forward to a due process hearing as well as the time and toll it takes on staff. After considerable dialogue, the parents, part of a well-known wealthy family in town, agreed to accept the offer of the per-pupil cost. When their decision reached the school committee, one member came to our office, very unhappy and upset with the agreement made with this particular family. We reminded the school committee member that the law requires a FAPE be provided to all eligible students—even those who reside in a wealthy household. We also informed the school committee member of our attorney's support for the agreement, understanding that had we moved to a due process hearing and not prevailed, we would be responsible for our attorney's fee, the full cost of the placement, transportation (which was not included in the agreement), and potentially the attorney's fees related to the parents' representation.

Our point is that ensuring your attorney looks at all aspects of a case is critical for you and for your school district. You may also need your attorney to review specific policies or procedures to ensure their alignment with all legal requirements such as discipline policies for students with special needs or review materials that you will send along to parents, staff, or administrators. The benefits of competent, sound legal advice and support will far outweigh the cost of the attorney's fees throughout the school year. One mistake can cost a district thousands of dollars and create an atmosphere of confusion and distrust for staff, the school district, and the community. Your appropriate reliance on legal consultation can assist you in a multitude of areas of concern and keep the district in compliance with all requirements.

Mediation

A parent or a school district may request mediation and/or a hearing at any time on any matter concerning a student's eligibility, evaluation, placement, IEP, or provision of special education services. Mediation can be an effective tool for both the school district and the parents of students with special needs. Mediation is a good-faith and confidential attempt to resolve any differences that arise between school districts and parents regarding how to proceed with services required that allow the student to receive a FAPE in the LRE. This differs from a resolution meeting where confidentiality is not stipulated so discussion can be brought forward at a due process hearing. See Appendix X for some do's and don'ts to consider before entering mediation. Understand that the goal of mediation is for the school district and the parent to come to some mutual agreement regarding the disputed recommendations of the student's IEP. The process is not perfect and does not prevent parents from seeking a hearing as part of the due process. As indicated, however, discussion at mediation cannot be brought forward as part of the record at a due process hearing because both parties have agreed to keep the mediation session confidential. Mediation *can* bring about a reasonable settlement in which the district and parents agree to some form of action that protects the child and the parents. The mediated agreement may relieve the school district from the burden and expense of a hearing that could lead to additional costs for the district in attorney fees, tuition for out-of-district placement, and potential transportation cost. The mediation setting also allows you to establish a relationship with parents and build trust that the district shares their objective in providing their child with the best educational services possible.

It is important to recognize the benefits of mediation. This tool can lead to resolution and actually build trust and faith on the part of the parents in the district's ability to compromise. We found that offering to attend mediation was an effective approach to assist parents in recognizing the district's work in the best interest of their child. Less formal than a hearing, the mediation process allows for give and take with the mediator acting as the arbitrator, serving both parties. Yes, this usually means that give and take must occur on the part of both parties to achieve success, which means that you as the ASE must keep an open mind and relinquish some of your authority and control, as must the parents, to reach an agreement. This can be, and often is, difficult for many administrators, but getting to "yes" (Fisher & Ury, 1981) is far better than getting to "no," simply based on control. Remember we have been speaking of serving in the best interests of students, so an open mind must be part of your toolbox.

Your skills as a communicator are essential in working toward a mutually agreed-upon outcome. Seemingly simple things like knowing when to table something for discussion and when to hold back or when and how to ask a question for positive clarification are strategies to consider that can bring about positive resolution. We have listed some helpful communication leads in Appendix II that may assist you with preparing to listen, communicate, clarify, and work toward resolution at a mediation. We always understood the importance of designating a single spokesperson to represent the district, and we saw that as our role. We would gather as much information as possible regarding a student by reviewing the student's file, visiting the student's classroom, observing the student in unstructured settings like recess and lunch, and speaking to all staff servicing the student. It was not unusual for either of us to attend a mediation alone, and if issues came up that we had not anticipated, we would ask to reconvene and gather the needed data. We always wanted to keep the dynamics of the session to a minimum as we never knew what staff might bring up or how they might respond. We used this time to attempt to rebuild some of the trust that the parents may have lost in the school district, and we felt not including staff kept the parents *away from* any confrontation and *with* their students. Moving to a hearing would require them to be away from their students for an extended period of time. We also wanted parents to view the disagreements as with us, not with any staff members who might be involved should the matter move forward.

We attempted to keep the focus of the mediation on effective progress, FAPE, and LRE. As mentioned in Chapter 1, *Board of Education of the Hendrick Hudson Central School District v. Rowley*, 458 U.S. 176 (1982), defined effective progress as education reasonably calculated to allow the student to be promoted from grade to grade. The case of *Endrew F. v. Douglas County School District*, 580 U.S. ___ (2017), has expanded that language to include education reasonably calculated to allow the student to progress given the individual circumstances of the student. This new language of "individual circumstances" requires clarification as you go into due process as advocates and attorneys may well seek to draw this statement into the issues discussed.

Hearings

When the parties fail to resolve their differences regarding the rejected IEP for the student, the next option available is a full due process hearing. If either of the parties has not been represented by counsel, this is generally the time in the process that attorneys get involved. The average hearing lasts five days and the cost of an attorney is on average $1,500-plus per day, so the hearing alone would cost a minimum of $7,500, not including prep, post-hearing briefs, or fees for the parent's attorney should the district not prevail. A key factor in making the decision to proceed to a hearing is the toll the process takes on staff; they have not received any training on what to expect and what to anticipate once the attorneys get involved—that is, time away from their students for hearing preparation, time away from their students for the hearing, and the impact of cross-examination by the opposing attorney. Keep in mind attorneys, both yours and the parents', get paid to win. A hearing officer once explained the process as beginning with a blank slate, followed by each party being given the opportunity to submit exhibits, call witnesses, and cross-examine witnesses.

The hearing officer, a neutral party, then reviews the entire record and renders a decision either indicating that the plan as presented by the district was adequate for the student or ordering required changes to the IEP that will make it appropriate for the student. A hearing is remarkably similar to a trial as both sides have the right to call witnesses and present evidence. Remember that the rules of evidence may be unique to your state. Our state, for example, has a specific rule called the five-day rule by which copies of all documents to be introduced (exhibits) and a list of all witnesses to be called at the hearing must be received by the opposing party (or parties) and the hearing officer at least five business days prior to the hearing unless otherwise allowed by the hearing officer. So, you need an attorney who can counsel you on all significant timelines and aspects of the process in your state.

Briefs and interrogatories cover an array of questions related to the student's teacher and others serving the student as well as what services are being provided and how. As that hearing officer once described it to us, the student's parents and the school district are responsible at the hearing to fill in a blank slate through testimony and exhibits that will allow them to weigh the evidence and render a decision. In our state, as indicated in previous chapters, the statistics related to hearing decisions historically show 50 percent favoring parents and 50 percent favoring school districts. This always reminded us that as good as we believed our services or program to be, moving forward to a hearing had at best a 50/50 chance of ending in our favor.

CHAPTER SUMMARY

Due process is part of the legislation of special education. A hearing can be and most often is a trying experience for all involved, be they school personnel or parents. As we have discussed, agreement through a resolution meeting with the parents or mediation is most desirable. School districts are charged with the burden of proof when entering due process through a hearing. The issue is not black-and-white; many factors play into the decision to go to hearing, such as strength of the program or service, credibility of witnesses, and impact on staff, all of which can cost the district in so many ways. It is most important to focus your actions on getting everyone to "yes" and doing what is best for the students you serve than to fight like hell only to not prevail at a hearing, lose the parents' confidence, and develop the reputation of a fighter, simply for the sake of the fight.

If you have quality staff and quality defensible programs, then, yes—you need to take appropriate action when disagreement occurs between you and the family, but not as a first resort. You must review all aspects of the case and make a sound judgment based on the data, the evidence, the skills of your staff, and the progress of the student. Once you review the data, you can decide on the best course of action.

This process will be stressful for you as well as your staff. No one ever got into servicing students in special education with the expectation of being cross-examined by an attorney or seeing their résumé put under a microscope. Your primary role throughout this process is to support your staff and reassure them of their expertise in the field. We have spoken about employing solid counsel—trust your attorney. Don't allow yourself to lock into your position; your attorney's role is to assess the evidence and advise you accordingly, so listen to their advice!

Conclusion

Keys to Becoming a Successful Administrator of Special Education

Have you asked yourself why you are aspiring to be an administrator of special education (ASE) or, if you are in the position, why you took the position? Is it to have a better-paying job, more authority, a step to becoming a superintendent or assistant superintendent, or all of these? Or, are you doing it to make a difference in the lives of students and parents or staff? These are important questions to reflect on as you take on the daunting task of administering a special education program. Not only will you be the leader of your department, but you will also be the manager of your department. As noted throughout the book, your beliefs and values must always drive your decision making and the direction of your department.

Several colleagues of ours were known to overmanage and were never able to separate their role as a manager from their role as a leader. Leadership and management are not the same thing. Leadership and management are complementary, but it is important to understand how they differ.

Leadership is about vision and innovation; this involves your vision for your program structure as well as for how your beliefs and expectations will be seen and utilized throughout your district. Management is where you go about maintaining the standard of excellence you espouse to. Still another way to look at leadership and management is that a leader innovates, and a manager administrates on the innovation.

It is important to remember that you are the face of special education in your district and often the message you need to send is not a popular one. You may need to inform a principal or staff member why they cannot do something the way they want to, or a parent that the district is not responsible to provide a specific service or assessment. Or you may need to inform your superintendent of a new legal mandate, a regulation change, a new placement, or some other requirement that they may not want to hear. A former colleague of ours attended a retirement party and sat next to his former superintendent, who said to him, "I owe you an apology." "What do you mean?" our colleague asked, and the superintendent informed him that when he came into his office, he never saw the person; he saw a green book (the regulations were green at that time), and he knew he was about to be told something that required a difficult scenario or would cost a lot of money. We have mentioned your being a "professional flack catcher" and how difficult that is to adjust to; well, the same can be said for being the face of special education—anyone in the community not pleased with some aspect of special education visualizes you as the one to blame.

On the occasion that you are required to make a presentation to your school committee, keep a few things in mind and always be prepared— remember the five *P*s!—for anything. You may be presenting on a specific topic; however, you are also a captive audience, and any issue or concern that a committee member might have been thinking about may be presented to you for reaction. On the many occasions that we made school committee presentations, the obvious goal was to be comprehensive and to never have a committee member asking for more. In our preparation, we would go through all our difficult cases, budget items, building issues, state directives, and on and on, reminding ourselves that any topic would be fair game once discussion of our primary topic was concluded. We always rehearsed our presentation or a specific response prior to any school committee meeting. If you are required to attend all school committee meetings and you are not presenting, prepare yourself anyway, because if your experience is anything like ours, you will on many occasions be called upon to address an issue or answer a question that may have grown out of an ongoing discussion. When unable to give a response, don't hesitate to indicate that you need to follow up and will get back to the individual committee member, or the whole committee if need be, in a timely manner.

Your state Department of Education is a valuable source of information, and also the overseer of your district's compliance with the law. Our experience has shown us that when the department conducts a compliance review, they are looking to see if the district has "crossed all the *t*s and dotted all the *i*s"; they are not looking at the quality of your programs or the instruction you are providing to students. They enter your district with the intention of determining whether your district has met all timelines, translated all documents, conducted three-year reevaluations, and so on and, if not, to determine your action plan and timeline to do so. You will never hear your Department of Education asking that you train staff in the Wilson Reading System, the Orton-Gillingham Approach, Lindamood Phoneme Sequencing (LiPS), the Stevenson Reading program, or Fundations. Our default was always to give the department as little as possible—if they require more, they will let you know. We also refrained from asking them questions as we saw many of our colleagues receive answers they were not prepared to hear. Rather, we believed in doing what needed to be done, as we saw it appropriate, and if they disagreed at some point, they were welcome to tell us and then we would change our approach.

As you take on this job, many aspects can and likely will be daunting, as mentioned. You may be entering a district where the same person led the department for many years, and everyone is looking for you to keep everything the same or for you to make what they believe are needed changes. Be leery of the staff who come to your door in the early days with advice on how things should be. There may be personnel matters to address, but be patient. Starting in your office, look at how staff members communicate, how the mail is handled, and how phone calls are answered; simply put, observe and absorb. Perhaps your leadership style will be different from your predecessor's, and if that is the case, you will need to establish your expectations for and with staff. You may want to consider developing an Entry Plan as many superintendents do when entering a new district. You may inherit staff members who do their own thing and have become accustomed to having it their way. Again, be patient and observe and develop how you want to conduct the difficult conversation. And remember to always conduct these conversations behind a closed door. It is possible that the union will get involved early on as you go about establishing your expectations.

As new ASEs, we found it most productive to seek out the union leadership to introduce ourselves and let them know that although we were not predicting it, staff might not accept our expectations and might as a result seek union assistance. If you see that as a possibility in your role as ASE, you must let the union leaders know; as we state throughout this book, no one likes to be blindsided. We have said for years that the students are rarely the problem—it is generally the adults. Your job is to provide these adults, be it staff or parents, with the training and knowledge they require and, as stated earlier, when difficulties arise, to go behind a closed door to address whatever they may be.

We have covered many areas that we consider necessary to establish a strong framework for your success. Here is a starting point and a summary of what we consider significant areas that will assist and guide you in the position of ASE:

LISTEN. The ability to listen is a gift and takes a lot of hard work to master. Each of us believes that we have answers to most situations that arise; after all, we are the administrator. In reality, any veteran administrator will tell you that they do not have most of the answers; they listen to everyone and assess the best way to proceed. Your insight may come from a parent, a teacher, a principal, a secretary, or even the custodial staff depending on the issue that needs to be addressed.

BE VISIBLE. This job is very demanding, and you can find yourself confined to your office and attending meetings all day, every day. If you get a call from a teacher or a principal, go to the school, and let them know that you are there to assist them and that you care about the students in their school. Believe us—principals have no idea what you do, and they might think that you are there to charge in and fix problems when they occur. And again, as you visit classrooms, spend time getting to know the students.

DEVELOP RELATIONSHIPS. Your credibility and the credibility of your department depends on the relationships you develop with significant individuals. The first place to start is the business office. Your budget, your grants, your staffing needs, and transportation all go through this office, and having a solid working relationship with the business manager and the staff in this office will make your life and theirs so much better.

KNOW YOUR MOST VOCAL CASES. Find out from your staff which cases have the most potential for concern and get involved. These cases can take a significant toll on the staff members involved, and if they believe that you are there to assist, then they can continue to provide the services needed in a quality manner.

STAY ON TOP OF YOUR BUDGET. This often may be the first thing you want to put on the back burner when it seems that everyone needs your attention and you have several volatile cases going on at the same time. *Do not* let this happen. Superintendents are not going to ask you how you are doing with those difficult cases or how things are going in general, but they *will* ask you how your budget is doing and what it looks like for the remainder of the year.

BE PUNCTUAL. No one wants to wait for you; as indicated, most everyone believes that you are sitting by the phone, waiting for their call, and they do not want to hear how busy you are. This goes for meetings, as well as returning phone calls, emails, and texts. Being punctual, or not, is one of the easier ways to either enhance or diminish your reputation.

MAINTAIN CONFIDENTIALITY. Nothing will compromise your credibility quicker than breaching confidentiality. When you need to speak to a principal, staff member, or parent, close the door and work out what needs to be worked out. If you agree to something, hold to it, and if confidence has been shared, *keep it confidential*.

EMBRACE PARENTS. Always remember that your student is their child! You may not agree with what they want or how they are proceeding, but you can let them know that you too want their child to succeed. Parents know their child better than anyone, and it is important to listen to their insight(s) and observation(s). You may disagree; however, it will lessen the possibility of the situation becoming adversarial if you let them know you respect their advocating for their child. Although the school district's Individualized Education Plan (IEP) may not be what they had wanted or expected, assure them that the school professionals also want the best for their child.

TRUST YOUR STAFF. Your staff are not the enemy. Your staff are the people in the trenches each day doing incredible work in service of their students with special needs. They will have great insight into the students when things are not working as they should, and they will also have great insight for you when it comes to addressing matters that involve their students deemed eligible for special education. In our state, Massachusetts, each IEP written must contain a statement on bullying and how the Team looks to address it should it be a focus for the student.

Positive Stories

As a "professional flack catcher," your days can be consumed with the negative. We have found that finding time to reflect and focus on the positive is a must. Over our careers, we developed many positive programs, hired quality staff, provided technology for students and staff to access, and much more. The positive thing that meant the most to us and has stayed with us over the years was witnessing the success of students, attending their graduations, and seeing the pride that they and their families exhibited. For example, we watched a student from one of our programs for those with hearing impairment go on to college and return to teach physical education at a local school for the deaf. We love going to the supermarket or clothing store or garden shop and encountering students we knew from years ago enjoying their work. We have not only seen students who received IEP services go on to college and succeed in their chosen field but actually hired some to teach special education or provide an itinerant service. Watching students turn into young adults and move on to be productive citizens, regardless of their disability, never gets old. Most importantly, all the "flack catching" did not get in the way of our getting out to the schools and into the classrooms where the real work of special education is conducted every day.

Appendices

Leadership Lessons From Geese by Joel Garfinkle

As leaders, we can learn a lot from the goose. Geese are intriguing creatures and while considered pests in certain situations, they also have an incredibly strong sense of family and group loyalty. Probably one of the most phenomenal geese facts is that their desire to return to their birthplace every year is so strong that they will often fly up to 3,000 miles to get there.

As you consider these fascinating facts, think about how you could apply these lessons to incorporate a bit of goose behavior into developing leadership skills to create your own style.

- **Fact 1:** As each goose flaps its wings, it creates an uplift for the birds that follow. By flying in V formation, the whole flock adds 71% greater flying range than if each bird flew alone.

  Lesson: People who share a common direction and sense of community can get where they are going quicker and easier, because they are traveling on the thrust of one another.

- **Fact 2:** When a goose falls out of formation, it suddenly feels the drag and resistance of flying alone. It quickly moves back into formation to take advantage of the lifting power of the bird immediately in front of it.

  Lesson: If we have as much sense as a goose, we stay in formation with those headed where we want to go. We are willing to accept their help, and we give our help to others.

- **Fact 3:** When the lead goose tires, it rotates back into the formation and another goose flies to the point position.

Lesson: It pays to take turns doing the hard tasks and sharing leadership. As with geese, people are interdependent on each other's skills, capabilities, and unique arrangement of gifts, talents, or resources.

- **Fact 4:** The geese flying in formation honk to encourage those in front to keep up their speed.

  Lesson: We need to make sure our honking is encouraging. In groups where there is encouragement, the production is greater. The power of encouragement (to stand by one's heart or core values and encourage the heart and core of others) is the quality of honking we seek.

- **Fact 5:** When a goose gets sick, wounded, or shot down, two geese drop out of formation and follow it down to help or protect it. They stay with it until it dies or is able to fly again. Then they launch out with another formation or catch up with the flock

  Lesson: If we have as much sense as geese, we will stand by each other in difficult times as well as when we are strong.

This was transcribed from a speech given by Angeles Arrien at the 1991 Organizational Development Network, based on the work of Milton Olson.

APPENDIX II

Important Aspects of Listening

HEARING: Merely implies that sounds have been received.

Does not indicate that comprehension or retention has taken place.

LISTENING: Requires hearing, comprehension, and retention of the material presented.

Good Listening Habits

- Prepare to listen.
- Take responsibility for comprehending.
- Listen to learn and understand, not to argue.
- Pick out main ideas.
- Practice control of the emotions.
- Keep an alert mind.
- Write down key ideas.

Good Listening Habits

- The Golden Rule—listen to others as you would have them listen to you.
- Use the speaker's name when addressing them.
- Look at the speaker.
- Concentrate on the words.
- Be courteous if you disagree.
- Do not interrupt.

Distinguish Between Main and Secondary Ideas

- Listen carefully to beginning remarks.
- Pay special attention to ideas covered at length.
- Listen for key words.
- Pay close attention to the conclusion.
- Learn to distinguish between fact and opinion.

Helpful Communication Phrases

It is important that we be continuously open-minded and cautious in appraising others, consider most judgments as tentative, and remember that at best we will have a limited understanding of the unique person with whom we are interacting.

Some phrases that are useful when you trust that your perceptions are accurate, and the person is receptive to your communications, might be:

- You feel . . .
- From your point of view . . .
- It seems to you . .
- In your experience . . .
- From where you stand . . .
- As you see it . . .
- You think . . .
- You believe . . .
- What I hear you saying . . .
- You are . . . (identify the feeling; for example, angry, sad, or overjoyed)
- I am picking up that you . . .
- I really hear you saying that . . . Is that where you are coming from . . . ?
- You figure . . .
- You mean . . .

Some phrases that are useful when you are having some difficulty perceiving clearly, or it seems that the person might not be receptive to your communications, might be:

- Could it be that . . . ?
- I wonder if . . .
- Correct me if I am wrong, but . . .
- Is it possible that . . . ?
- Does it sound reasonable that you . . . ?
- Could this be what is going on? You . . .
- From where I stand, you . . .

- This is what I think I hear you saying . . .
- You appear to be feeling . . .
- It appears you . . .
- Perhaps you are feeling . . .
- I somehow sense that maybe you feel . . .
- Is there any chance that you . . . ?
- Is it conceivable that . . . ?
- Maybe this is a long shot, but . . .
- I am not sure if I am with you; do you mean . . . ?
- I'm not certain I understand; you're feeling . . .
- It seems that *you* . . .
- As I hear it, you . . .
- . . . Is that the way it is?
- . . . Is that what you meant?
- . . . Is that the way you feel?
- Let me see if I understand; *you* . . .
- I get the impression that . . .
- I guess that you are . . .

APPENDIX III

Haim Ginott

"I've come to the frightening conclusion that I am the decisive element in the classroom. It is my personal approach that creates the climate. It is my daily mood that makes the weather. As a teacher, I possess tremendous power to make a student's life miserable or joyous. I can be a tool of torture or an instrument of inspiration. I can humiliate or humor, hurt or heal. In all situations it is my response that decides whether a crisis will be escalated or de-escalated, and a student humanized or de-humanized."

APPENDIX IV

Confidentiality

To: All Special Education Personnel

From: XXXXXX, Special Education Administrator

Date:

Re: CONFIDENTIALITY

The Department is required to inform staff annually of their responsibilities regarding confidentiality of student information. The Student Record Regulations/FERPA allow only authorized school personnel to have access to information in a student's record. Authorized school personnel are defined as school administrators, teachers (to include therapists), and counselors (to include school psychologists) who are employed by the district and who are working directly with the student. Individuals not working with a student do not have access to the record without the written permission of the parent or student (age 14 or entering Grade 9).

The most appropriate way to proceed with confidential records or information about a student is to ask ourselves how we would want someone to deal with the information if it was information about our own child or ourselves.

Staff who are interested in additional information relating to the student records can access it at XXXXXX.

Thank you for your attention to this most important subject.

APPENDIX V

Alphabet Soup

Acronyms Related to
Special Education and Other Special Services

688	Massachusetts Turning 22 Transition Law
766	Massachusetts Special Education Law
ADA	Americans With Disabilities Act
ADD	Attention Deficit Disorder
ADHD	Attention Deficit Hyperactivity Disorder
AYP	Adequate Yearly Progress
BIP	Behavior Intervention Plan
CAPD	Central Auditory Processing Disorder
CBA	Curriculum-Based Assessment
CD	Conduct Disorder
DCAP	District Curriculum Accommodation Plan
DD	Developmental Disability
ED	Emotional Disturbance
EHA	Education of All Handicapped Children Act
EQA	Education Quality Assurance
FAPE	Free and Appropriate Public Education
FAS	Fetal Alcohol Syndrome
FBA	Functional Behavioral Assessment
HI	Hearing Impairment
ID	Intellectual Disability
IDEA	Individuals With Disabilities Education Act
IDEA-97	Reauthorization of IDEA
IEP	Individualized Education Plan
IFSP	Individualized Family Service Plan
LD	Learning Disability
LRE	Least Restrictive Environment
MCAS	Massachusetts Comprehensive Assessment System
NCLB	No Child Left Behind
NLD	Nonverbal Learning Disability
OCD	Obsessive Compulsive Disorder
ODD	Oppositional Defiant Disorder

OHI	Other Health Impairment
PDD	Pervasive Developmental Disorder
PL 94-142	First Federal Special Education Law
PTSD	Post-Traumatic Stress Disorder
PQA	Program Quality Assurance
SIP	School Improvement Plan
TAT (SAT)	Teacher Assistance Team (Student Assistance Team)
TBE	Transitional Bilingual Education
VI	Visual Impairment

APPENDIX VI

Timelines (Massachusetts)

Referral and Evaluation

TIMELINES

1. *Initial Referral.* When a student is referred for an evaluation to determine eligibility for special education, the school district shall send written notice to the student's parent(s) within **five school days** of receipt of the referral.

2. *Upon Referral.* School districts **shall evaluate children who are two and a half years of age** and who may be receiving services through an early intervention program. An initial evaluation shall be conducted to ensure that if such child is found eligible, special education services begin promptly at age three.

3. *Initial Evaluation.* Upon consent of a parent, the school district shall provide or arrange for the evaluation of the student by a multidisciplinary team **within 30 school days**.

   1. Summaries of assessments shall be completed prior to discussion by the Team and, upon request, shall be made available to the parents at least **two days in advance of the Team** discussion at the meeting occurring pursuant to 603 CMR 28.05(1).

   - **Convening the Team. Within 45 school working days** after receipt of a parent's written consent to an initial evaluation or reevaluation, the school district shall provide an evaluation; convene a Team meeting to review the evaluation data, determine whether the student requires special education, and, if required, develop an Individualized Education Plan (IEP) in accordance with state and federal laws; and provide the parents with two copies of the proposed IEP and proposed placement, except that the proposal of placement may be delayed according to the provisions of 603 CMR 28.06(2)(e); or, if the Team determines that the student is not eligible for special education, the school district shall send a written explanation of the finding that the student is not eligible. The evaluation assessments shall be completed **within 30 school working days** after receipt of parental consent for evaluation. Summaries of such assessments shall be completed to ensure their availability to parents at least two days prior to the Team meeting. If consent is received within

30 to 45 school working days before the end of the school year, the school district shall ensure that a Team meeting is scheduled so as to allow for the provision of a proposed IEP or written notice of the finding that the student is **not eligible no later than 14 days after the end of the school year**.

- **Annual reviews and three-year reevaluations**. The school district shall review the IEPs and the progress of each eligible student at least annually. Additionally, every three years, or sooner, if necessary, the school district shall, with parental consent, conduct a full three-year reevaluation consistent with the requirements of federal law.

- **Unscheduled evaluations for medical reasons**. If, in the opinion of the student's physician, an eligible student is likely to remain at home, in a hospital, or in a pediatric nursing home for medical reasons and for more than 60 school days in any school year, the administrator of special education shall, **without undue delay,** convene a Team to consider evaluation needs and, if appropriate, to amend the existing IEP or develop a new IEP suited to the student's unique circumstances.

- **Independent education evaluations**. Upon receipt of evaluation results, if a parent disagrees with an initial evaluation or reevaluation completed by the school district, then the parent may request an independent education evaluation.

  - The parent may obtain an independent education evaluation at private expense at any time.

  - The right to this publicly funded independent education evaluation under 603 CMR 28.04(5)(c) continues for **16 months from the date of the evaluation with which the parent disagrees**.

  - Whenever possible, the independent education evaluation shall be completed and a written report sent **no later than 30 days after the date the parent requests the independent education evaluation**. If publicly funded, the report shall be sent to the parents and to the school district. The independent evaluator shall be requested to provide a report that summarizes, in writing, procedures, assessments, results, and diagnostic impressions as well as educationally relevant recommendations for meeting identified needs of the student. The independent evaluator may recommend appropriate types of placements but shall not recommend specific classrooms or schools.

Within 10 school days from the time the school district receives the report of the independent education evaluation, the Team shall reconvene and consider the independent education evaluation and whether a new or amended IEP is appropriate.

APPENDIX VII

Reminders

- Always be cognizant of **time**.
- Do not talk about individual students in front of them.
- Do not make offhanded comments to parents.
  - ○ Think before you speak.
- Never say there is no money to cover something.
- Do not pass judgment on others.
  - ○ Parents.
  - ○ Students.
  - ○ Colleagues.
- Do not make promises you cannot keep or have no control over.
- **Prepare.**
  - ○ Prior Preparation Prevents Poor Performance.
- **Document! Document! Document!**
- Do not make recommendations for your colleagues.
  - ○ **Always** remain within your own area of expertise.
- **Never be afraid to ask for advice.**
- **Communicate!**
  - ○ No one likes to be blindsided.
    - ▪ Not parents, not colleagues, and not your students.
- Do not view parents as the enemy.
  - ○ Remember you are working with their child.
    - ▪ Always respect a parent's desire to advocate for their child . . .
      - • Even if you disagree with how they go about it.
- Always, always, always be professional.
- As you ask your students, take time to check your work.
  - ○ Communications with parents.
  - ○ Progress reports.
  - ○ Individualized Education Plans (IEPs).
  - ○ And more.

- Take time to review students' files.
  - Do not allow yourself to be in a position of saying to a parent:
    - "I haven't had time to review the file."
    - "I didn't know that"—particularly when the information is important and in the student's file.
- Establish professional relationships with:
  - Students.
  - Parents (refrain from addressing them by first name; using *Mr.* and *Ms.* makes for a nice professional relationship).
  - Colleagues.
  - Teachers.
  - Specialists.
- **And *remember*, if you bring coffee to a meeting, be sure to bring enough for everyone, or do not bring it at all**.

APPENDIX VIII

Superintendent Survey Responses

	HIGH	LOW
Overview of legal requirements	14	7
Special education discipline	11	8
Special education finances		
Budget	13	9
Tuitions	10	10
Transportation	5	13
Grants	9	12
Procedural safeguards	12	5
IEP process and development	5	15
Identification of disabilities	5	14
Inclusive practices	13	7
Development of special education programs	14	8
Parent involvement	5	11
Professional development considerations	14	5
Roles of various special education personnel	7	11
What do I need to know from my ASE?	13	9
What is my role overseeing special education?	11	9

APPENDIX IX

Decorum Standards for Special Education Team Meetings and Special Conferences

Purpose

The following standards for adult behavior at school-based meetings are provided as a guide for all adults who attend a meeting regarding students with special needs. It is the intent of these standards to assist in establishing a tone of collaboration and cooperation regarding the needs and issues that bring individuals to the meeting to discuss a particular student's status. An atmosphere of professional collegiality will enhance the discussion and move the discussion toward what is in the best interest of the student. The focus of the discussion is and must be the needs of the student.

Decorum Standards

- All parties agree to be on time for the scheduled meeting. Any delays should be preceded with a telephone call, email, or text to the student's school or designated meeting chairperson.

- Individuals who are unable to attend the scheduled meeting will provide the earliest possible notice to the designated meeting chairperson.

- Written request for student information will be given two days in advance of the meeting to the designated meeting chairperson to allow time for production of the documents. No later than twenty-four hours should be honored.

- Written documentation that is being provided by non-school personnel should be provided to the designated meeting chairperson.

- Introductions will be made by the designated meeting chairperson, and an overview will be given by this individual. The chairperson will review the purpose of the meeting, salient points that need to be identified, and the actions, steps, accommodations, interventions, and other moves that have been made. Other issues or points that meeting participants want to identify will be made at this time. The order of presentation will be determined by the meeting chairperson, and exceptions due to time constraints or other issues will be noted and honored.

- Background information will be kept to the salient points and will be focused on the reason for the meeting.

- Presenters need to stay focused on the issues and be allowed to complete their presentation without interruption. Clarifying questions can and should be asked at the conclusion of the presentation. It is the chairperson's responsibility to recognize all those who want to ask questions and to facilitate dialogue in a positive, productive manner.

- Should any individual be unable to maintain appropriate and respectful adult behavior, the chairperson will remind that individual of the decorum standards and inform the individual that should they continue to act in a disrespectful manner the meeting will be adjourned. The meeting chairperson has the option to recess the meeting for a brief period to allow an individual to regain composure.

- Any meeting that is adjourned will be rescheduled, and a notice will be sent to all meeting participants of the new meeting date and time of the reconvening of the meeting.

Conclusion

It is the intent of these guidelines to establish an atmosphere of respect and collegiality that will enhance the dialogue and lead to a positive conclusion for the student. Through everyone's cooperation, it is believed that school-based meetings can and will be a positive productive experience for all participants.

APPENDIX X

Mediation Strategies

Prior to Mediation

DO:

- Negotiate only with those in power or authorized delegates.
- Deal from strength, which comes from preparation.
- Know the true needs of the other parties.
- Bargain for accommodations rather than win or "wipe out."

DON'T:

- Underestimate the other side.
- Overestimate yourself, your team, the justification of the case, or strategies.
- Wait to prepare.
- Talk loosely about plans or attitudes.

During Mediation

DO:

- Keep an open mind.
- Bring your ideas about what can be done to improve the situation.
- Take some time to assess carefully. In assessing alternative options for students with special needs, it is important to think about *why* a particular option may be a better match for the child. What are the elements of a program that may contribute to a successful educational experience for the child?
- Focus on the match between this child's progress and the suitability of the program for this child. Keep an open mind to the array of services that are available.
- Think about the present and the future.
- Try to develop a coordinated and coherent understanding of the child's needs.
- Make your comments in a way that helps the parent see their child as a whole person, rather than as a consumer of specific services.
- Be prepared to consider new options.

- Be sure you know the current reality when it comes to available services and personnel.
- Be calm and cool.
- Be personable, and use people's names; be respectful.
- Be confident—in yourself and in the process.
- Be flexible.
- Listen carefully.
- Keep a poker face.
- Take command of meetings without verbal domination. Keep meetings on track, focused on the issues at hand. Sell your ideas persistently.
- Defer discussion on key issues.
- Phrase questions for a positive response.
- Study alternatives and new information.
- Caucus often, but do not keep people waiting too long.
- Be the first to bring up major issues.
- Avoid intimidation.
- Respect confidentiality.
- Express appreciation of others' time and effort.

DON'T:

- Start out putting the parent on the defensive by reviewing all the things that you perceive have gone wrong in the past.
- Forget that every child is different. Talking about other children who *seem* like this child may not be truly helpful.
- Become so committed to a single way of doing things that you do not recognize a good opportunity when it is presented to you.
- Get trapped by previous experiences, which may be outdated, or which may apply to other children but not this child.
- Focus on past dissatisfactions. Recognize that you have long-term interests in the development of this child.
- Argue among yourselves; save it for the caucus.
- Lose your temper.
- Waste people's time.
- List priorities for the other side.

- Escalate demands or present surprises.
- Oversell.
- Compromise your objectives or philosophies.
- Let your guard down.
- React too unfavorably, assign blame, or interrupt—this turns people off.
- Wait to spill bad news.
- Rush the other side.
- Be pressured; if you have doubts, delay.
- Be afraid to let an issue stay on table.
- Keep worrying about the end result.
- End meetings on a negative note.

AND DO NOT EVER:

- Make promises you cannot keep.
- Lie.
- Bluff.
- Trick.
- Assume.

IF YOU SETTLE:

- Be sure the agreement captures all agreed-upon items.
- Be sure the language of the agreement is clear.

IF YOU DO NOT SETTLE:

- Be respectful.
- Remember—your student is the parent's child, not yours.
- Reiterate that although no agreement was reached, both sides are only looking out for the best interest of the child.

Acknowledgments

We would both like to acknowledge our deceased parents who laid the foundation for our beliefs about children in need.

To the superintendents we worked with throughout our careers—Dr. Charles Lamontagne, Dr. Daniel G. O'Connor, Dr. Sally Dias, Paul Andrews, Marsha McDonough, and Dr. Joseph Connelly—we learned from each of you and treasured your direction and support.

To our Corwin team—Jessica, Melanie, Melinda, Mia, Natalie, Olivia, Ricardo, and Lucas—you made this experience so enjoyable, and we clearly could not have done this without you.

We were both fortunate to have secretaries who were always watching out for us: Mary Palmer, Ruth Delong, Carol Brewster, Dottie Curtis, Diane McCarthy, Diane Patterson, Gail Prive, Mary Negri, Patricia Walsh, Patricia Shaughnessy, Janice LoPrete, Joan Keene, Marilyn Micco, Mary Marchant, and Barbara Stewart.

So many names, so little space. A note of grateful appreciation to all the staff whom we worked with and hired over our careers. You assisted us with the work that we did and do, ensuring that students with special needs received the social, emotional, and academic opportunities and experiences that were most appropriate for them. We both had the great pleasure of working with many talented and dedicated teachers, paraprofessionals, speech pathologists, therapists, school psychologists, school counselors, secretaries, custodians, and cafeteria workers. We want to thank, as well, the many school committee members, school administrators, and central office administrators who supported our efforts and strengthened our resolve to do the very best for students. To those who mentored and coached us—Jim Anderson, Hank Owen, Bill (Willie) McDonough, Dr. Jim Bradley, Paul Antonellis, Dr. Gary Siperstein, Bill Ferris, Veronica Andrews, and so many others—they clearly shaped our career direction, and to Dr. Robert Rotondo for his life-altering vote.

We also had the opportunity to interact with many pioneers of these new laws who provided us with foundational guidance that contributed to our development as administrators of special education.

And to the students and parents we came to know, we hope you know that we always had your best interests to guide our efforts.

References

American Psychiatric Association. (2013). *The diagnostic and statistical manual of mental disorders* (5th ed.). American Psychiatric Association.

Barker, J. (1989). *The business of paradigms* (Original version). Star Thrower Distribution. https://starthrower.com/products/the-business-of-paradigms-original-joel-barker

Bateman, D., & Cline, J. (2012). *Special education leadership: Building effective programs in schools.* Routledge.

Berman, S. H., & Urion, D. K. (2003, March). The misdiagnosis of special education costs. *School Administrator, 60*(3). https://www.aasa.org/SchoolAdministratorArticle.aspx?id=9248

Berne, E. (1964). *Games people play: The psychology of human relationships.* Grove Press.

Bittel, P. J., & Young, N. D. (2012). *Transforming special education practices.* Published in partnership with the American Association of School Administrators and Rowman & Littlefield Education, a division of Rowman & Littlefield Publishers, Inc.

Bragar, M., Tagliareni, S., & Palames, C. (1979). *Section 504: An action guide for secondary school administrators.* Developed with the assistance of the Massachusetts Department of Education.

Burrello, L. C., & Sage, D. D. (1979). *Leadership and change in special education.* Prentice Hall.

Crockett, J. R., Billingsley, B., & Boslandin, M. L. (2012). *Handbook of leadership and administration for special education.* Routledge.

Davis, K. (1967). *Human relations at work*: The dynamics of organizational behavior. McGraw-Hill.

Earle, J., & Clark, S. G. (2001). Lessons learned from special education leadership, development knowledge, diffusion and schools as organizations. *Electronic Journal for Inclusive Education, 1*(4).

Fisher, R., & Ury, W. (1981). *Getting to yes: Negotiating agreement without giving in.* Houghton Mifflin.

Freedman, M. K. (2017). *Special education 2.0.: Breaking taboos to build a new education law.* School Law Pro.

Freedman, M. K. (1995, February 15). The elevator theory of special education. *Education Week.* https://www.edweek.org/teaching-learning/opinion-the-elevator-theory-of-special-education/1995/02

Fullan, M. (2008). *The six secrets of change: What the best leaders do to help their organizations survive and thrive.* Jossey-Bass.

Harkins, S. B. (2012). Mainstreaming, the Regular Education Initiative, and inclusion as lived experience, 1974–2004: A practitioner's view. *Inquiry in Education, 3*(1). https://files.eric.ed.gov/fulltext/EJ1171834.pdf

Havelock, R. G. (1973). *The change agent's guide to innovation education* (2nd ed.). Educational Technology Publications.

Hehir, T. (2005). New directions in special education: *Eliminating ableism in policy and practice.* Harvard Education Press.

Hehir, T., Grindal, T., & Edelman, H. (2012, April). *Review of special education in the Commonwealth of Massachusetts* (Report commissioned by the Massachusetts Department of Elementary and Secondary Education). Thomas Hehir and Associates. https://www.doe.mass.edu/sped/hehir/

Heifetz, R. A., & Linsky, M. (2002). *Leadership on the line: Staying alive through the dangers of leading.* Harvard Business School Press.

Lavoie, B. (1989). *How difficult can this be? The F.A.T. City Workshop* [Video]. PBS. https://www.ricklavoie.com/videos.html

Lentz, K. (2021). *Transformational leadership in special education*: Leading the IEP team. Rowman & Littlefield.

Lieberman, L. M. (2001, January 17). The death of special education. *Education Week.* https://www.edweek.org/teaching-learning/opinion-the-death-of-special-education/2001/01

Maggin, D. M., & Hughes, M. T. (2021). *Developing teacher leaders in special education: An administrative guide to building inclusive schools*. Routledge.

Maslow, A. (1954). *Motivation and personality*. Harper.

Massachusetts Department of Elementary and Secondary Education. (2015). *Educator effectiveness guidebook for inclusive practice*. Massachusetts Department of Elementary and Secondary Education.

Massachusetts Department of Elementary and Secondary Education. (2001). *Massachusetts dyslexia guidelines*. https://www.doe.mass.edu/sped/dyslexia-guidelines.pdf

Massachusetts Department of Elementary and Secondary Education. (1980). *Chapter 71B, Chapter 766 regulations* (4th ed.). Massachusetts Department of Elementary and Secondary Education.

Moscovitch, E. (1993). *Special education: Good intentions gone awry.* Pioneer Institute for Public Policy Research.

Schultz, J. (2011). *Nowhere to hide: Why kids with ADHD and LD hate school and what we can do about it.* Jossey-Bass.

Stone, D., & Heen, S. (2014). *Thanks for the feedback: The science and art of receiving feedback well.* Penguin Group.

Stone, D., Patton, B., & Heen, S. (2000). *Difficult conversations.* Penguin Books.

Wehman, P. (2019). *Essentials of transition planning* (2nd ed.). Brookes Transition to Adulthood Services.

Widener, R. E., Jr. (2011). *Evaluating special education teachers: Do we get the job done?* Electronic Theses and Dissertations. East Tennessee State University School of Graduate Studies. https://dc.etsu.edu/cgi/viewcontent.cgi?article=2478&context=etd

Wilcox, G., Conde, F., & Knowbel, C. (2021). Using evidence-based practices and data-based decision making in inclusive education. *Education Science,* 11(129).

Wurzberg, G. (Director), & Goodwin, T. C., Wurzberg, G., & Nevins, S. (1992). *Educating Peter* [Video]. HBO Direct Cinema Limited.

Index

A SAGE Publishing Company

Helping educators make the greatest impact

CORWIN HAS ONE MISSION: to enhance education through intentional professional learning.

We build long-term relationships with our authors, educators, clients, and associations who partner with us to develop and continuously improve the best evidence-based practices that establish and support lifelong learning.

Solutions YOU WANT | Experts YOU TRUST | Results YOU NEED

INSTITUTES

Corwin Institutes provide regional and virtual events where educators collaborate with peers and learn from industry experts. Prepare to be recharged and motivated!

corwin.com/institutes

ON-SITE PROFESSIONAL LEARNING

Corwin on-site PD is delivered through high-energy keynotes, practical workshops, and custom coaching services designed to support knowledge development and implementation.

www.corwin.com/pd

VIRTUAL PROFESSIONAL LEARNING

Our virtual PD combines live expert facilitation with the flexibility of anytime, anywhere professional learning. See the power of intentionally designed virtual PD.

www.corwin.com/virtualworkshops

CORWIN ONLINE

Online learning designed to engage, inform, challenge, and inspire. Our courses offer practical, classroom-focused instruction that will meet your continuing education needs and enhance your practice.

www.corwinonline.com

PLSN20YA8

CORWIN